sushi modern

THE ESSENTIAL KITCHEN

sushi modern
HIDEO DEKURA

PERIPLUS

contents

sushi modern

sushi modern

In Japanese writing, *sushi* is written as one character: the left part of the character means "fish," and the right part means "delicious" or "good." Often mistakenly described as raw fish, because of the traditional inclusion of some type of fish, sushi is defined as the combination of vinegared rice with other ingredients.

Sushi Modern presents sushi as an edible art form, exploring new ideas, and creative arrangements and combinations of common ingredients that make sushi a truly modern food.

Sushi was adopted more than a thousand years ago in Japan as a method of preserving fish with rice. It is believed that sushi originated in Southeast Asia as a technique called *nare-zushi*. This process involved preserving cleaned raw fish, which were pressed between layers of salt and rice and weighted down with a stone. After a few months, the rice was discarded and the fermented fish was considered ready to be consumed. The flavor of the fish is so strong, often obscuring its identity altogether, that it is something of an acquired taste.

During the eighteenth century, a chef named Yohei in the Edo region (which is, coincidentally, the former name for Tokyo) decided to forgo the fermentation process of *nare-zushi* and instead served the rice and fish in something resembling its present form of *nigiri-zushi*, sushi rice topped with fresh raw fish. This style of sushi became very popular, and two distinct styles emerged in Japan: the Kansai style, from the city of Osaka in the Kansai region, which produced nori rolls and molded sushi with a sweeter-tasting sushi rice; and the Edo style, from Tokyo, which is hand-shaped sushi with a seafood topping.

The immense popularity of sushi in Japan meant that other regions developed their own distinctive styles of sushi, which exist today, with each region differing in the method of preparation and in the shape and the taste of the sushi.

However, the worldwide popularity of sushi has meant that it is no longer exclusive to Japan, and while maintaining its uniqueness, sushi styles have continued to change. Over the last two decades, the ways of preparing sushi, in Japan and worldwide, have evolved to include new and modern creations that utilize an incredibly wide variety of ingredients, including shellfish, vegetables, chicken, beef, and pork. Only rice has remained the essential ingredient, although this book explores ways in which the rice can be varied or replaced.

Once, not many people would have considered eating sushi without soy sauce or wasabi, but there is a wide range of other sauces and accompaniments that works well with sushi in their place. As our world becomes smaller and the availability of food increases dramatically, these days we also find ingredients combined in sushi that had not previously been dreamed of. Asian ingredients such as cilantro (fresh coriander), Thai basil, chili, fish sauce, and coconut have flavors that are very compatible with sushi.

Creating new or unique styles of sushi is possible—just let your taste be the judge. Once you acquire the basic skills for making traditional sushi, you can modify the taste to produce sushi that you feel comfortable with and excited about offering to family and friends. This book is designed to help you expand your ideas about sushi.

The number of Japanese shops and restaurants has increased remarkably over recent years. There is now a huge range of sushi restaurants, from those offering economical sushi on plates on conveyor belts (or "sushi trains") to five-star sushi-bars. Sushi bars can provide great ideas for the home cook, as they often combine traditional sushi with new ingredients and techniques. But after trying some of the recipes in this book, you may say to yourself that your own homemade sushi is the best of all.

Sushi can be eaten with chopsticks, a fork and a knife, or the hands. Nigiri-zushi (hand-shaped sushi) is mostly eaten using the fingers, and each diner is provided with a damp hand towel beside their plate to clean their hands. Since nigiri-zushi is formed without over-compressing the sushi rice, it is better to use the fingers as opposed to chopsticks as there is a chance the rice may crumble before it reaches your mouth. When eating nigiri-zushi, dip the top ingredients rather than the sushi rice into the soy sauce, as the sauce will cause the rice to lose its shape. Nigiri-zushi is designed to be eaten in one bite, without causing a mess, so when making nigiri-zushi, make sure they are bite-sized.

Cone sushi, or hand rolls, are eaten with the fingers. Rolled sushi and inside-out rolled sushi are eaten with the fingers or chopsticks. Chirashi-zushi (scattered sushi) is eaten with chopsticks, or a spoon or a fork can be used instead. A fork is often more suitable for molded sushi.

It can be said that sushi is the Japanese equivalent of the Western sandwich: a portable, staple food that can be served simply or dressed up for special occasions, and there is no limit to the variations that can be created. One bite gives you a combination of the distinctive sweet and sour flavors of sushi rice, the tang of wasabi, a selection of fillings, and the added zest of soy.

Is it *sushi* or *zushi*? The correct Japanese word for a vinegared rice roll is *sushi*. However, in the Japanese language, when two nouns are joined together to form a word, the first sound of the second word may change its vocal quality. Hence *inari* (bean curd wrapper) plus *sushi* becomes *inari-zushi*.

Chopsticks

Fingers

Knife and fork

Types of sushi

Nigiri-zushi

The English meaning of *nigiri*—hand-shaped—is a little misleading, since most sushi is shaped by hand. However, it is a historical term from the time when sushi was a method of preserving fish by pressing it with rice. *Nigiri-zushi* evolved in Tokyo in the early nineteenth century, when fish and shellfish was plentiful in nearby Tokyo Bay. The general term *sushi* is often used to refer to nigiri-zushi. However, nigiri-zushi specifically consists of a piece of fish or shellfish placed on an oblong-shaped finger of lightly vinegared rice, and usually seasoned with a dab of wasabi. As a topping, tuna, snapper, octopus, freshwater eel, salmon roe, shrimp, squid, tuna belly, sweet shrimp, sea urchin, or salmon may be used.

Maki-zushi: Large sushi rolls

Maki-zushi refers to handmade sushi that encloses some filling inside a roll of nori-wrapped rice. It is often shortened to nori maki. There are various types of nori make.

Futomaki-zushi: Thick sushi roll

Futomaki-zushi is thick nori maki made with a full-sized sheet of nori (seaweed), spread evenly with a layer of vinegared rice and enclosing several fillings and sometimes a dab of wasabi. A large variety of fillings may be used, such as crisp vegetables, seafood, omelette, and pickles, making it a very tasty, versatile type of sushi.

Hosomaki-zushi: Thin sushi rolls

Hosomaki-zushi is a thin sushi roll that uses a half-sheet of nori with less sushi rice and a single filling. For the novice sushi-roll maker, it is easier to make than a thick sushi roll.

Inside-out California roll

As the name suggests, the rice is on the outside of this roll rather than the inside. Sometimes the rice may be decorated with tobikko (flying fish roe), which can be orange, green or golden in color; toasted white or black sesame seeds; or tempura flakes.

Molded sushi

Molded sushi is traditionally made with a Japanese mold that comes with an insert that allows for easy removal. Without one of these molds, it is best to make the sushi in simple shapes, as sticky sushi rice can be difficult to remove from more detailed molds.

Temaki-zushi: Hand roll/cone sushi

Temaki-zushi is another type of sushi roll that is cone-shaped or log-shaped. It is called a hand roll, as it is usually constructed at the table (or perhaps at a picnic) by the person who is going to eat it. Hand rolls are made from a selection of fillings, along with sushi rice, and each one is rolled into quartered sheets of nori to form a cone that is eaten by hand.

Chirashi-zushi: Scattered sushi

This is the easiest type of sushi to make, as it is simply sushi rice with other ingredients mixed in or placed over sushi rice served in a bowl. Traditionally, the topping included a variety of fish and/or shellfish, but these days a mixture of vegetables is also quite common. It is sometimes included in lunch boxes.

Wrapper sushi

Wrapper sushi refers to sushi rice wrapped in foods other than nori. The best known wrapper sushi is *inari-zushi*, in which the wrapper is a pouch of sweetened tofu (bean curd) called *inari*. In Japan's Kansai region, fresh young Japanese persimmon leaves are often used as a wrapper.

New sushi

Using the basic techniques for making traditional sushi, you may create your own style, limited only by your imagination.

Nigiri-zushi

Maki-zushi: Large sushi rolls

Hosomaki-zushi: Thin sushi rolls

Inside-out California rolls

Molded sushi

Temaki-zushi (hand roll/cone sushi)

Chirashi-zushi (scattered sushi)

Wrapper sushi

New sushi

Modern sushi is a versatile, adaptable, and convenient food, because it can be made from a variety of ingredients that are readily available in local and Asian markets and in your kitchen pantry. The choice is unlimited and includes fresh vegetables, meats, poultry, dairy products, Asian herbs, and fresh or dried fruit.

The basic ingredients of sushi are short-grain rice, rice vinegar, mirin, nori sheets, wasabi paste, and soy sauce. All of these are available in supermarkets. However, specific Japanese ingredients such as inari may only be available from Japanese and Asian markets.

Sushi rice is essential for most sushi, as the stickiness of this kind of rice is necessary for molding sushi into shapes. In this book, vinegared couscous is introduced as a substitute for rice, but, because the grains of couscous contain less starch than rice, it is not used for shaped sushi. If you wish to vary sushi rice in any hand-molded or rolled sushi, it is best to do so by adding color, for example through the use of ingredients such as black rice (colored rice), beet (beetroot) juice, or saffron.

Wasabi paste is commonly used in sushi to provide a tangy flavor, but it also can be substituted. Condiments such as horseradish sauce, particularly red horseradish sauce, English or French mustard, or chili paste can replace wasabi. If using chili paste, make sure it is not too hot.

Recently, Japanese mayonnaise has become a popular accompaniment to sushi in Japan. In this book, variations such as vinaigrette sauce and green curry paste are introduced as accompaniments.

Though herbs are not commonly used in traditional sushi, they are an interesting addition to modern sushi. Chives, basil, mint, and Japanese basil (shiso), which is available from Japanese markets during the summer months, are all good choices.

The glossary in the following pages illustrates some of the ingredients used throughout this book.

Nori: Use toasted nori for sushi

Rice vinegar

Sushi rice

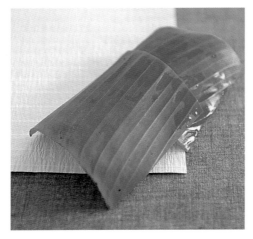

Banana leaf

Inari (beancurd pouches)

Mirin

Cream cheese

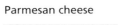

Parmesan cheese

Anchovies

Canned crab, salmon, and tuna

Prosciutto and salami

Smoked salmon

Sun-dried tomatoes and capers

Apple mint

Avocado

Baby spinach

Cilantro (fresh coriander)

Daikon (Japanese radish)

Dill

Dried mango

Edible flowers

Eggplants (aubergines)

Green beans

Kaiware (radish sprouts)

Kinome (Prickly ash)

Mushrooms: Shiitake and enoki

Mustard cress

Shiso (Japanese basil)

Thai basil

Ruby grapefruit

The following utensils and equipment will save time and energy when making sushi.

Bamboo sushi mat (sudare)

A bamboo sushi mat is made of thin bamboo strips stitched together to form a mat that can be rolled. They are available in several sizes. Small mats, which are approximately 4 inches (10 cm) square, are used for hand-rolled sushi. Large mats are approximately 12 inches (30 cm) square and are used for the thicker sushi rolls. Extra-large mats are also available to make super rolls, but these are not covered in this book. After using a sushi mat, rinse well with water to remove any food particles, and let it dry completely before storing in a cool, dry place.

Cooking chopsticks (saibashi)

Saibashi are made of bamboo and are longer than those used for eating. Their length allows for better handling of food when cooking.

Knives (houchou)

Sushi knives are as important to a chef as a sword is to a samurai. The knives are made from carbon steel that can be sharpened to cut a single hair. A chef's set of sushi knives can cost several hundred dollars apiece. They are sharpened before and after use, cleaned after every few strokes, then wrapped, and stored in a safe place. Unlike most knives, sushi knives are sharpened on one side only, which makes for a faster, cleaner cut. There is now a variety of knives designed especially for sushi and sashimi preparation available in local knife shops. Japanese knives are available in Japanese stores or large Asian grocery stores. Also, a new style of knives is available from kitchenware stores.

Leaf decoration (baram or haram)

Leaf decorations may be used to separate sushi rolls on a plate or in a lunch box. Bamboo and aspidistra leaves are most suitable, as they can be cut into shapes such as grass blades, birds (cranes, in particular), and so on.

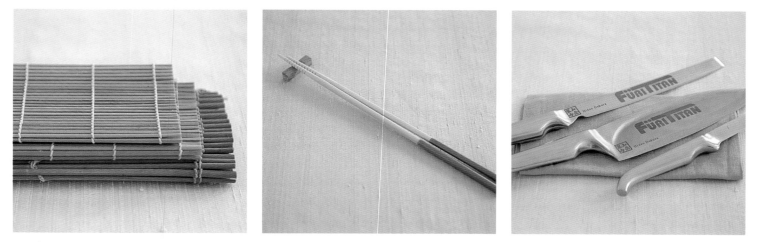

Bamboo sushi mat   Cooking chopsticks   Knives

Leaf decoration

Molds

Rice cooker

Rice paddle and wooden sushi bowl

Sauce bottles

Teacup and teapot

Tempura pan

Vegetable cutters

Vegetable peeler

Molds (sushi kata)

Japanese sushi molds can be plastic, wooden, or metal, and of various shapes. They have a separate insert with a handle, which is used to press down on the rice to mold it into shape, and to enable the outer mold to be easily removed.

Rice cooker (suihanki)

A good rice cooker is a great time-saver. It produces perfect rice every time, and it turns off automatically, so you never have burnt rice.

Rice paddle (shamoji) and wooden sushi bowl (hangiri)

The Japanese rice paddle is a wide, flat wooden or plastic paddle which is used with a slicing, rather than a stirring action, to lift and aerate the rice while it is being cooled with a hand-held fan. Wooden or bamboo spatulas, readily available in kitchenware departments, may be substituted.

A wooden bowl helps to draw away excess moisture as sushi rice cools down. However, a large wooden bowl is an expensive item and not easily obtainable. A plastic or china bowl can be substituted.

Sauce bottles (sousu no bin)

A small sauce bottle for condiments, such as soy sauce, is a necessary inclusion in a lunch box. They are sold at Japanese markets or other Asian stores.

Teacup and teapot (kyusu to yunomi)

Nowadays, Japanese teacups and teapots can be found in most kitchenware shops. The most pleasing teapot and teacups are fine porcelain. Japanese teapots have a very fine-mesh strainer, which is either built into the base of the spout or is part of a removable basket. They are small compared to Western teapots. In sushi bars, Japanese tea is served in a deep, narrow pottery cup with no handle, which may be inscribed with the logo of the sushi bar. However, smaller cups are used at home.

Tempura pan (tempura nabe)

A tempura pan has fairly straight sides, that are approximately 4 inches (10 cm) deep. It has a removable wire-mesh draining rack attached to the pan, which keeps the cooked tempura warm and allows the oil to drain. A wok can also be used, and some also have a draining rack.

Vegetable cutters (kata)

Flower-shaped cutters are available from Japanese stores. Cookie cutters may be substituted.

Vegetable peeler (kawamuki)

The Japanese peeler is similar to a potato peeler, but the blade is set at a right angle to the handle, which makes it easy to slice vegetables in thin, long strips that are suitable for making wrapper sushi.

Step-by-step knife sharpening

A traditional Japanese knife differs from a Western knife by being beveled on one side only. Hence, most Japanese knives are designed for right-handed people. Left-handed knives are available for left-handed users. If you are unable to find a Japanese knife at a shop near you, try the Internet.

For knife sharpening, you will need 2 damp towels, a whetstone (such as a diamond stone), and water. Before sharpening a Japanese-style knife, soak the whetstone in water for about 20 minutes.

1. Place a pre-soaked whetstone on a damp towel to hold it in place. Moisten surface of stone with water. Wipe clean with a damp towel and hold knife in your right hand. Place top half of blade flat on stone at a 45-degree angle to your body. Placing middle and index fingers of your left hand on blade, apply pressure and move blade forward and backward. Wipe blade.

2. Once the top is sharpened, repeat with base of blade.

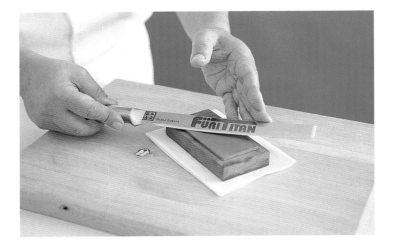

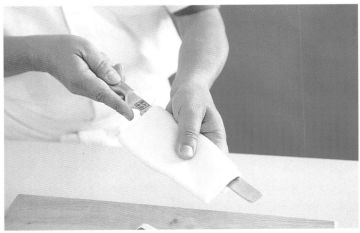

3. As most Japanese knives are single-edged, when blade is honed shaved pieces will cling to flat side of blade. To remove, turn knife, and place edge of blade on edge of stone at a 45-degree angle. Slide blade down to remove excess metal.

4. Wipe knife clean with a damp towel.

fish and shellfish

Choosing fish

The most effective way of making sure you choose the freshest fish for sushi is to approach your local fishmonger or sushi chef to find out where to buy sashimi-grade fish.

Fresh fish has a sheen to it and is not dull, the eyes are sparkling, it has a pleasant sea smell, and the flesh is firm to the touch. Also, you should check that the gills are pink, not blackened, in color. If you have to travel a distance to obtain the fish, be prepared to transport it in an insulated cooler (or eski). Use ice packs as opposed to ice cubes, because the water from the ice will ruin the fish.

Types of fish cuts for sushi

Most varieties of fish cuts are suitable for sushi. The fish pieces may be raw, grilled, or preserved in vinaigrette. Fresh raw fish for sushi include salmon, snapper, king fish, yellowtail, John Dory, and tuna.

Shellfish is also suitable. Most shrimp (prawns) are cooked before being used as sushi toppings. Fresh lobster has a wonderful texture and a natural sweetness that makes it very suitable for sushi, though it may be too expensive for everyday use. You may prepare a lobster yourself, or purchase fresh or frozen lobster tails, for use in sushi.

Eel is available filleted and barbecued with sweet soy sauce from the frozen-food section of most Japanese and some other Asian markets. Before using as a sushi topping, steam the eel, or heat it slightly in the microwave, then slice into sushi-sized pieces.

Mackerel is the most popular fish for preserving in vinaigrette as a sushi topping. In one region of Japan, rice and mackerel sushi are wrapped in Japanese persimmon leaves to enhance the flavor.

Tasty fish eggs, such as caviar and tobikko (flying fish roe) and sea urchin roe, add a dramatic decorative effect to sushi, as well as a distinctive taste sensation.

Nowadays, even processed fish products are becoming popular, such as processed crabmeat (kani kamaboko) which is a common ingredient used in California rolls and hand rolls or sushi cones. Also, canned fish such as tuna, mixed with Japanese mayonnaise, is quite popular among the youth of Japan.

Step-by-step filleting fish

In this filleting illustration (opposite), a king fish is used. The utensils needed are a chopping board, a sharp filleting knife, and a clean kitchen towel. Other medium-sized fish, such as snapper, salmon, or bonito, may be substituted for king fish.

Fish such as snapper must be scaled before filleting. If scaling is required, wipe the knife occasionally with a clean cloth to avoid shredding the flesh.

This three-part filleting process yields two fish fillets. The skeleton and tail are discarded.

Preparing cooked sushi rice

¹/₂ cup (4 fl oz/125 ml) rice vinegar

2 tablespoons sugar

pinch of salt

You will need a wooden sushi bowl and rice paddle, or a wooden salad bowl and a wooden spatula, to make the sushi rice. A nonmetallic bowl and paddle are preferable, as the vinegar in sushi rice can react with metal and cause an unpleasant taste.

1. After rice is cooked and rice cooker has switched off, leave for 20 minutes to steam rice. When rice is ready, combine rice vinegar, sugar, and salt in a small bowl. Wipe inside of wooden bowl with a damp cloth to moisten slightly.

    Moisten rice paddle with water. Using a dry cloth to hold rice cooker in case it is very hot, transfer rice to center of bowl using rice paddle.

2. Slowly pour vinegar dressing over rice and loosen rice to separate grains, slicing paddle across bowl, rather than stirring, and spread rice evenly around bowl using rice paddle.

3. While continuing this process, fan mixture either with a hand-held fan, or an electric fan set on low, to cool rice as it absorbs vinegar mixture. This produces a glossy finish to rice. Continue until rice is lukewarm.

4. Spread a damp muslin cloth or kitchen towel over rice, and cover with a lid until ready to use.

Note: Do not refrigerate cooked sushi rice, as this causes the gluten to congeal, which reduces the stickiness and makes it hard to shape properly, as well as lessening the flavor. Cooked sushi rice will not keep for more than 1 day.

Sushi rice is called *shari*, which means "a tiny piece of Buddha's bone," because of the resemblance of its shape and preciousness of its nature. Making it requires practice. Good sushi rice has a delicate balance of sweet and sour, firmness and stickiness, and it shines like a pearl.

The measurements of sugar and vinegar are seasonal and regional. In Japan, in the summer, a little more vinegar is used, and in western Japan, sushi is sweeter than in the eastern part. All the measurements can be adjusted to suit personal taste.

3 cups (21 oz/655 g) short-grain rice

3 tablespoons black rice

3 cups (24 fl oz/750 ml) water

1 tablespoon mirin

1/2 cup (4 fl oz/125 ml) rice vinegar

2 tablespoons sugar

pinch of salt

Combine short-grain rice and black rice in a medium bowl. Cover with a lid. Rinse and soak rice, then cook, following instructions on page 20. Let rice sit, covered, in the rice cooker or pan for 20 minutes to steam rice.

Combine rice vinegar, sugar, and salt in a small bowl. Wipe the inside of a wooden rice bowl with a clean damp muslin cloth or kitchen towel. Moisten a rice paddle with water. Using a dry cloth to hold rice cooker with your hand in case it is very hot, transfer rice to center of bowl with rice paddle.

Gradually pour vinegar dressing over rice while loosening rice to separate grains, by slicing paddle across bowl, rather than stirring. Spread rice evenly around bowl, using a rice paddle.

While continuing this process, fan mixture with either a hand-held fan, or an electric fan set on low, to cool rice as it absorbs vinegar mixture. This produces a glossy finish to the rice. Continue until rice is lukewarm.

Spread a damp muslin cloth or a kitchen towel over rice, and cover with a lid until ready to use.

Makes about 6 cups (30 oz/940 g)

Tip

Black rice is available at Asian markets. It resembles wild rice in shape and color and adds color to the other ingredients with which it is cooked.

Transfer rice to center of bowl with rice paddle

Pour vinegar dressing over rice

Spread rice evenly around bowl with rice paddle

Prepared black rice

hosomaki-zushi

These thin sushi rolls are easy to make, as usually only one type of filling is used. Although the amount of filling is quite small, the variety of fillings that may be used is endless. You can select ingredients from your pantry, refrigerator, or freezer, and use fillings such as canned tuna, salami, cheese, and avocado.

It is best to have all ingredients and equipment needed for making sushi handy. This includes a bamboo sushi mat and a small bowl of water with a splash of rice vinegar to dip your hands in and keep the rice from sticking to them.

1 cup (5 oz/150 g) prepared sushi rice (pages 20–21)

1/2 sheet nori

wasabi paste to taste

1 small English (hothouse) cucumber, seeded and cut lengthwise into 4 sticks, each about 1/2 inch (6 mm) thick

1. Trim the sides of a halved nori sheet. Place a bamboo sushi mat on a dry work surface and lay nori on mat, glossy side down. Set nori in center of mat, about 1¼ inches (3 cm) away from edge of mat closest to you. Wet your hands, and take a small handful of rice. Spread rice evenly over nori, leaving uncovered a ¾-inch (2-cm) strip of nori on the side farthest from you. Dab a small amount of wasabi on your finger and spread thinly across center of rice. Top wasabi with fillings of choice, such as cucumber strips.

2. Using your index finger and thumb, pick up edge of sushi mat nearest to you. Place your remaining fingers over fillings to hold them as you roll mat forward tightly.

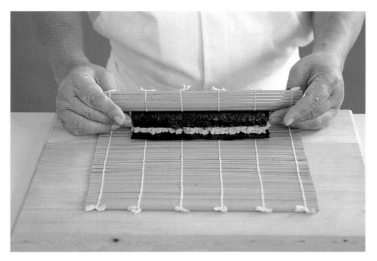

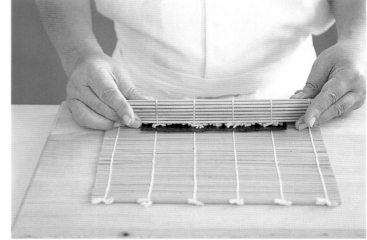

3. Roll the mat, wrapping rice and nori around fillings. The strip of nori without rice should still be visible.

4. Lift up top edge of mat and continue rolling sushi roll over rice-free portion of nori, encasing roll within the mat. If nori is dry, moisten edge of rice-free strip of nori with your wet fingers.

5. With a gentle press on bamboo mat, form sushi as if molding a rectangular bar with the fingers.

6. Remove mat, and transfer sushi roll to a dry cutting board. Wipe knife with a damp towel and slice roll in half. Place 2 pieces side by side and cut them in half again to make 6 rolls, wiping knife after each cut.

hand rolls

California cone rolls

2 sheets nori

2 cups (10 oz/300 g) prepared sushi rice
(pages 20–21)

$1/2$ teaspoon wasabi paste

4 tablespoons (2 oz/60 g) Japanese mayonnaise

fillings of choice, such as 4 sticks crabmeat
($3/8$ inch x 2 inches/1 x 5 cm),

4 avocado slices

4 English (hothouse) cucumber slices

Makes 4 rolls

These do-it-yourself hand-rolled sushi cones are an easy and fun way for family and guests to make their own sushi. This technique not only allows diners to choose their preferred fillings, but to also vary the combinations to suit their personal taste. People of all ages and abilities, including children, can create hand rolls. Prepare the ingredients beforehand, placing them on a platter or in individual bowls. Give your guests guidance on technique, and then let them make their own. Hand rolls should be eaten as soon as made as they do not hold well. Prepare a finger bowl with water for each person and provide warmed, dampened towels for guests to wipe their hands on.

To help beginners avoid making a mess with the rice, start with smaller quantities of rice and ingredients and increase quantities as they gain confidence in rolling. If your guests would enjoy more fillings and less sushi rice, use quartered nori sheets to make small cone rolls.

1. Cut nori sheet in half. Hold nori flat in your left hand, glossy-side down. Wet fingers of your right hand, and take about 1 tablespoon of rice and spread it evenly on the left side of nori. Add a small amount of wasabi and Japanese mayonnaise to rice.

2. Arrange crabmeat, avocado, and cucumber sticks in the center of rice.

3. Fold bottom lefthand corner of nori over fillings and tuck it under rice, allowing the top to open out somewhat. Roll the remainder of nori sheet into a cone-shaped sushi roll.

4. To seal nori, use a little water.

There are a number of different ways sushi can be served, including as an entrée, or as an entire meal consisting of many different varieties. A "roll-your-own" party is another possibility, and sushi is always a welcome treat at picnics.

In planning a sushi meal, consider the following points.

First, sushi is best eaten immediately after rolling. This is also one of the best things about rolling your own sushi cones. As it may not always be possible to make sushi just before guests arrive, prepare all the ingredients required beforehand and make sushi the last item of preparation for the meal. It is best not to leave sushi ingredients, at room temperature, for more than 2–3 hours before using. Raw fish will require refrigeration. To keep sushi rice fresh for a day, cover with a clean muslin (cheesecloth) and keep in a refrigerated container without any ice. Do not refrigerate.

Second, refrigeration changes the quality of sushi rice. It reduces its starchiness and stickiness, and the rice can become quite hard. For this reason, sushi rice should be kept at room temperature, for no more than 1 day.

Finally, if raw fish is used, the finished sushi should not be allowed to stand at room temperature for too long. For this reason, it is important to consider the weather, as raw fish may not be appropriate on hot summer days.

A sushi platter may be served for an entrée in a similar manner to an Italian antipasto platter. The platter can include hand rolls, hand-shaped sushi (nigiri-zushi), and possibly inside-out sushi with gari (pickled ginger), wasabi, and leaf decorations. It is best to prepare the platter no more than 1 hour before consuming. As sushi is decorative in appearance, arrange rolls attractively to showcase its artistic qualities. Individual plates of sushi, with about 4 pieces per serving, can also make an attractive and fast entrée.

Hand-roll party
Do-it-yourself hand rolls allow the party organizer to simply prepare the ingredients and enjoy the rest of the party. If making sushi for a children's party, you may choose special ingredients, excluding wasabi for example. If using raw fish, remove it from the refrigerator at the last minute, place it on a bed of ice, and cover with a bamboo sushi mat.

Picnic
If a picnic is planned, a lunch box including sushi is a pleasant alternative to sandwiches. Because of possible spoilage, it is better not to use raw fish for picnics. Suggested ingredients are omelettes, cooked shrimp (prawns), avocado, smoked salmon, fresh vegetables such as cucumber and carrots, pickles, and cheese. They should be kept in a refrigerated container until ready to consume. Small plastic bottles are good for soy sauce and other essential dipping sauces. Alternatively, prepare the ingredients and wrap them separately in plastic wrap, then have family or friends roll their own sushi cones.

Main meal
Sushi can be prepared as a main meal in a similar fashion as an entrée by serving more substantial amounts of a variety of sushi, attractively displayed, on a large platter. Don't forget to provide individual dishes for dipping sauces.

Desserts
Gelatin desserts, pieces of fresh fruit, or sorbet are perfect treats after a sushi meal. They are light and refreshing, and provide a good balance to the sushi.

Do-it-yourself hand-roll party

Picnic

Main meal

Dessert

accompaniments

Drinks

Chrysanthemum flower tea

In Japan, fresh chrysanthemum flowers are used in sashimi, tempura, and soup. Chrysanthemum tea can also be made by pouring hot water on a couple of dried flowers. Combining it with a small amount of green or black tea helps to moderate the strong flavor. The flowers are available from Japanese or other Asian markets.

Green tea

In sushi bar terms, green tea is called *agari*, which means "a finish." In between sushi varieties, green tea is drunk to cleanse the palette to aid diners to appreciate the flavor of the next sushi roll. Green tea is the national beverage of Japan. Once the leaves of the tea bushes are picked, they are immediately steamed. This prevents the leaves from turning black, so the result is green tea. The syllable *cha* on the end of a word (or *ocha,* when it stands alone) means "tea."

There are a number of varieties of green teas, such as gyokuro, sencha, bancha, matcha (powdered green tea), genmaicha, and hojicha. The most economical tea is bancha; *bancha* means "late harvest" and is made from large, hard leaves, including the stems and red stalks. Because the flavor is weaker, it is suitable for children. Sencha is available in a wide variety of qualities and prices. Average-quality sencha of the large leaf variety is intended for everyday use and is commonly found in homes and offices. Gyokuro is the very best of Japan's teas. It has a delicate flavor that epitomizes the uniqueness of Japanese flavor. Depending on quality, the water temperature and length of infusion should be adjusted accordingly. Genmaicha is bancha made with hulled rice kernels, which adds an interesting flavor. These are both medium-quality teas that yield a light brown, refreshing infusion with a slightly savory flavor. It is rich in vitamins.

Hojicha

Hojicha was invented in 1920 by a merchant in Kyoto who did not know what to do with a surplus stock of leaves. He had the idea of roasting them and so created a tea with a new flavor. The lightly roasted leaves yield a light brown tea with a distinctive flavor.

Sake

Sake is the general word for all alcoholic beverages in Japan. However, it specifically refers to fermented rice wine, which is usually served in small porcelain cups. Sake is made by injecting a special mold (*Aspergillus oryzae*) into steamed white rice. The rice is fermented and then refined. The process takes 45–60 days from start to finish. Unlike Western wines, there is no aging. Sake is considered best to drink within three months of bottling.

Sake may be drunk at different temperatures. Nowadays, chilled sake is becoming popular in summer, though luke-warm (105°–120°F/40°–50°C) is the traditional temperature, and the usual way of ordering sake in Japan. This brings out the full flavor of the sake, which remains even after it has cooled. Hot sake (130°–140°F/55°–60°C) is great for winter. Sake is the perfect complement to sushi and other Japanese dishes that have the saltiness of teriyaki or soy sauce and the tang of wasabi.

Sauces and pastes

Aonori (seaweed) paste

Made from seaweed, this is particularly good with cooked rice. Sold in bottles in Japanese markets.

Chrysanthemum tea

Green tea

Hojicha tea

Sake

Aonori (seaweed) paste

Chili mayonnaise

Fish sauce

Green curry paste

Honey-chili sauce

Chili mayonnaise

This is chili added to Japanese mayonnaise. Use either chili paste or fresh chilies, and add as much or as little as desired. Chili mayonnaise is particularly suitable for chicken.

Fish sauce

Pungent sauce of salted, fermented fish and other seasonings, used in cooking and as a dipping sauce. Products vary in intensity based on the country of origin.

Green curry paste

This is suitable for sushi made with fresh vegetables or fruit.

Honey chili sauce

Available bottled from Asian or Japanese markets. Refrigerate after opening.

Japanese mayonnaise

Surprisingly, Japanese mayonnaise is suitable for a large variety of ingredients. It is less tangy than Western mayonnaise and is sold in a tube .

Mango chutney

This is a popular accompaniment to Indian curries. It has a sweet and sour taste and complements rice particularly well. Add to sushi in small amounts.

Pistachio and peanut sate sauce

This spicy, peanut-flavored sauce is a favorite in Indonesia. It is a mixture of peanut butter and crushed peanuts, sprinkled with chopped pistacho.

Soy sauce (Shoyu)

Soy sauce is essential to Japanese cuisine. Made from soybeans and salt, it is used in cooking and as a dipping sauce for sushi and other dishes.

Sweet and sour chili sauce

Available in bottles, from Asian markets, this is a very popular sauce in Asian countries. It is particularly suitable for pork dishes.

Wasabi

Wasabi is a native Japanese plant found growing near clear spring water. The root is grated and used as a condiment for sushi, sashimi, or soba noodles. Because of its distinctive pungent taste, it is often called Japanese mustard or horseradish. Wasabi is eaten with raw fish because it is believed to kill germs and parasites. It is available in both paste and powder forms.

As well as being used inside sushi rolls, wasabi can be served on the side. Its attractive green color lends itself to many decorative effects. Some people like to dip their sushi directly into the wasabi, but usually a small amount is picked up with chopsticks and mixed into a dish of soy sauce to use as a tangy dipping sauce.

Similar products with a "bite," such as chili or red horseradish sauce, may be used as a substitute for wasabi. It is best used sparingly, as the tang should add a subtle dimension to food and never dominate it.

Other accompaniments

Balsamic vinegar

Balsamic vinegar is a very versatile item to have in your pantry. It adds an extra zing to sushi salad rolls. Add by sprinkling the vinegar on the sushi rice, or dip salad vegetables in it prior to rolling.

Strawberry jam vinaigrette

This adds zest to vegetable sushi and sushi with dairy products (see page 88 for recipe).

Gari

The gari, or pickled ginger slices, that accompany sushi are for cleansing the palate in between dishes.

Japanese mayonnaise

Mango chutney

Pistachio and peanut sate sauce

Soy sauce

Sweet and sour chili sauce

Wasabi paste and powder

Balsamic vinegar

Strawberry jam vinaigrette

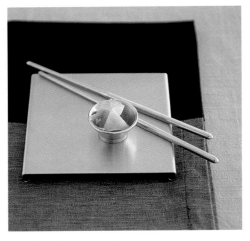
Gari (pickled ginger)

sushi rolls

Step-by-step shrimp tempura

8 medium shrimp (prawns), shelled and deveined
   (tails intact)
1 tablespoon katakuri starch or cornstarch
   (cornflour) for coating ingredients
1 cup (8 fl oz/250 ml) cold water
1 cup (5 oz/150 g) tempura flour (available from
   Asian markets)
canola oil for deep-frying
a few drops Asian sesame oil

Tempura is best eaten as soon as it is cooked. However, if you are using tempura as an ingredient in sushi, you should let it cool first.

Makes 8 pieces

1. Coat shrimp with katakuri starch and set aside. Mix equal amounts of cold water and tempura flour with chopsticks or a fork.

2. Fill a tempura pan, or deep-fryer one-third full with canola oil and add sesame oil. Heat over medium-high heat to 365°F (185°C), or until a small amount of tempura batter dropped into oil rises quickly to the surface, about 1 second.

3. Dip coated food into tempura batter and place it gently into oil. Deep-fry until it is golden brown, turning occasionally.

4. Using saibashi (or cooking chopsticks), remove tempura from oil and drain on wire rack for 30 seconds; then transfer to paper towels.

Golden rolls

TEMPURA FLAKES

1/2 cup (4 fl oz/125 ml) water

1/2 cup (2 1/2 oz/75 g) tempura flour

canola oil for deep-frying

a few drops Asian sesame oil

1/2 mango

1/2 avocado, pitted and peeled

1 nori sheet

1 cup (5 oz/150 g) prepared sushi rice (pages 20–21)

4 slices smoked salmon

1/2 teaspoon wasabi paste

To make tempura flakes, gently stir water and tempura flour together in a bowl until just mixed. Fill a tempura pan, or deep-fryer one-third full with canola oil. Add sesame oil. Heat over medium-high heat to 365°F (185°C), or until a drop of batter rises to the surface quickly (about 1 second). Using chopsticks or a fork, drop tempura batter into oil. Using a pair of dry chopsticks, divide flakes into small pieces as soon as they are dropped into oil. Fry until golden and crisp. Using a wire-mesh skimmer, remove to drain on a wire rack or paper towels, then transfer to paper towels and set aside.

Cut mango into strips, each 1/4-inch (6-mm) thick, then peel. Cut avocado into strips, each 1/4-inch (6-mm) thick. Place nori sheet, glossy side down, along end of sushi mat nearest to you. Spread sushi rice over nori, then cover with a large sheet of plastic wrap. Pick up mat, place a hand over plastic wrap, and carefully turn over so nori is on top. Place plastic, rice, and nori on mat about 3 slats from edge closest to you.

Place salmon slices in center of nori. Then, using your index finger, smear with wasabi. Place 3 strips of mango on top, then top with avocado. Tuck edge of plastic wrap under sushi mat. With hands supporting mat from underneath and pressing on ingredients with fingers, roll mat over ingredients, leaving a 3/4-inch (2-cm) strip at the end. Lift up mat, roll back a little, then roll forward to join nori edges. Gently press mat to form roll into a square shape, and seal. Unroll mat and transfer roll to a cutting board.

Wipe a sharp knife with a damp cloth and cut roll in half. Cut each half in half twice more to make 8 pieces, wiping knife after each cut. Gently remove plastic from rolls. Gently dip the outside of each roll into tempura flakes to give roll its golden color. It is better to add flakes to individual rolls, as flakes can become squashed during cutting.

Makes 8 pieces

California rolls with crabmeat and avocado

1¹/₄ nori sheets

¹/₂ avocado, pitted, peeled, and cut into strips, each ³/₈-inch (1-cm) thick

1 cup (5 oz/150 g) prepared sushi rice (pages 20–21)

1 tablespoon golden tobikko (flying fish roe)

1 tablespoon orange tobikko (flying fish roe)

1 tablespoon wasabi tobikko

¹/₄ English (hothouse) cucumber, cut lengthwise then into strips, each ¹/₄ inch (6 mm) thick

2 sticks crabmeat

Tip

Orange tobikko, the most popular of the three kinds of flying fish roe, is available from Japanese markets and fish stores. Wasabi and golden tobikko may be more difficult to find, but are available at speciality foods stores.

Place quartered nori sheet on a dry work surface, glossy side down, and place a strip of avocado in center of nori. Roll and set aside.

To make an inside-out sushi roll, place a whole nori sheet on a bamboo sushi mat, glossy side down, and spread sushi rice evenly over it. Using a teaspoon, spread golden, orange, and wasabi tobikko to create a striped pattern. Cut plastic wrap the same size as sushi mat and cover rice with mat. Pick up mat, place a hand over plastic wrap, and carefully turn over so nori is on top. Place back on mat about 3 slats from edge closest to you.

Place 1 slice avocado, 1 slice cucumber and 1 crabstick in center of nori. Using your index finger and thumb, pick up edge of sushi mat and plastic wrap nearest to you. Place remaining fingers over fillings to hold them as you roll mat forward tightly, wrapping rice and nori around fillings. Press gently and continue rolling forward to complete roll. Gently press mat to shape and seal roll. Unroll mat and transfer roll to a cutting board.

Wipe a sharp knife with a damp towel. Cut roll in half and cut the halves in half again; then cut each quarter in half to make 8 equal pieces, wiping knife after each cut. Finally, gently remove plastic wrap from each piece.

Makes 8 pieces

CALIFORNIA ROLLS WITH CRABMEAT AND AVOCADO

New Yorker rolls with spicy sirloin

canola oil for deep-frying

1 scallion (shallot/spring onion), finely shredded

1 carrot, peeled and finely shredded

FOR THAI BASIL SAUCE

1 tablespoon rice vinegar

1 teaspoon fish sauce

2 fresh Thai basil leaves, finely chopped

1 teaspoon packed brown sugar

1 tablespoon canola oil

2 oz (60 g) sirloin, thinly sliced

3/4 nori sheet

1 cup (5 oz/150 g) prepared sushi rice
  (pages 20–21)

2 fresh cilantro (coriander) leaves

1 clove garlic, crushed

1/4 teaspoon wasabi paste

Fill a tempura pan, or deep-fryer one-third full with canola oil and heat over medium-high heat to 365°F (185°C). Fry scallion until golden brown. Using a wire-mesh skimmer, transfer to paper towels to drain. Repeat with carrot. Set aside.

To make Thai basil sauce: Combine all ingredients in a bowl and mix well. Set aside.

Heat 1 tablespoon oil in a frying pan over medium heat, and cook sirloin, turning once, until rare, about 3 seconds. Transfer sirloin to a plate to cool.

Place nori on a bamboo sushi mat, glossy side down, and spread sushi rice over it. Place sirloin slices over three-quarters of nori, toward the front, and with wet hands spread sushi rice over sirloin. With your index finger, smear wasabi and garlic across center. Top with cilantro.

Using your index finger and thumb, pick up edge of sushi mat nearest to you. Place remaining fingers over fillings to hold them as you roll the mat forward tightly. Press gently and continue rolling forward to complete roll. Gently press mat to shape and seal roll. Unroll mat and transfer roll to a cutting board.

With a dampened knife, slice roll in half. Place 2 pieces side by side and cut them in half; then cut each half again to make a total of 8 pieces, wiping knife after each cut.

Top 4 pieces with fried onion and remaining 4 pieces with carrot. Serve with Thai basil sauce. Eat with chopsticks or fingers.

Makes 8 pieces

Tokyo rolls with aonori crepes

3/4 cup (4 oz/125 g) canned tuna, drained

2 tablespoons Japanese mayonnaise

2 eggs

1 teaspoon sugar

pinch of salt

1 teaspoon mirin

1 tablespoon aonori (nori) flakes

1 tablespoon canola oil

1 cup (5 oz/150 g) prepared sushi rice
 (pages 20–21)

wasabi paste to taste

1 English (hothouse) cucumber, cut lengthwise
 into 1/4-inch (6-mm) thick strips

4 nori strips, each 6 inches x 3/4 inch (15 cm x 2 cm)

8 gari (pickled ginger slices), drained

In a bowl, combine drained tuna and Japanese mayonnaise and mix well. Set aside.

To make crepes, whisk eggs, sugar, salt, and mirin together in a bowl. Add aonori flakes and stir lightly.

In a nonstick frying pan, heat oil over medium heat. Pour one-quarter of egg mixture into pan, swirling to coat the base. Cook until surface of crepe becomes dry. Turn crepe over and cook for 30 seconds. Transfer to a plate and cover. Repeat with remaining mixture to make 4 crepes.

Place 1 crepe on a dry work surface. With a wet hand, pick up about 1 tablespoon sushi rice and spread over center of crepe, in a triangular shape. Smear with wasabi. Spread tuna mixture over rice and place 2–3 cucumber strips on top. Fold edge of crepe over rice and roll up tightly into a cone shape (see page 26). Wrap a nori strip in a band around end. To seal nori, apply a little water along edge.

Serve with gari and soy sauce.

Make 4 cones

Tip

Aonori (flaked nori) is available from Asian markets, in packets or small bottles.

Cajun-style spicy rolls

4 smoked salmon slices

1 tablespoon cream cheese

1/4 teaspoon Cajun spice

1 cup (5 oz/150 g) prepared sushi rice
  (pages 20–21)

6 green beans, blanched

1 teaspoon shiso (Japanese basil) powder

Cover a sushi mat with plastic wrap. Lay salmon slices horizontally across plastic from edge closest to you. Spread cream cheese across center and sprinkle with Cajun spice. With wet fingers, spread sushi rice over salmon slices, leaving 3/4 inch (2 cm) uncovered. Place green beans in a straight line. Roll up very tightly following instructions on pages 24–25.

Unroll mat and transfer roll to a cutting board. Wipe a sharp knife with a damp towel, cut each roll in half, then cut each half into 4 pieces, wiping knife after each cut. Remove plastic from rolls.

Holding 1 piece, dip seam side into shiso powder. Arrange on serving plates. Repeat with remaining ingredients.

Makes 8 pieces

Tuna and salmon small rolls

1 can (4 oz/125 g) tuna in spring water, drained

2 tablespoons Japanese mayonnaise

leaves from 2 sprigs parsley, finely chopped

salt and pepper to taste

1 can (4 oz/125 g) salmon, drained

1 teaspoon red horseradish sauce

2 cups (10 oz/300 g) prepared sushi rice
  (pages 20–21)

1 nori sheet, cut in half

Put tuna in a bowl and use a fork to break up chunks. Add 1 tablespoon mayonnaise, parsley, salt, and pepper and stir to mix. Set aside. Put salmon in a bowl and use a fork to break up chunks. Add 1 tablespoon mayonnaise and horseradish sauce, and stir to mix.

Following instructions on pages 24–25, roll up nori and half sushi rice with tuna, parsley, and mayonnaise filling. Unroll the mat, remove plastic, and transfer the roll to a cutting board. Wipe a sharp knife with a damp towel and cut roll in half. Align rolls, cut in half again, then cut each slice in half once more, wiping knife after each cut.

Repeat with salmon and remaining sushi rice. Serve with soy sauce.

Makes 16 pieces

Tip

Shiso powder is available from Japanese and some other Asian markets.

CAJUN-STYLE SPICY ROLLS

Lobster tempura rolls

FOR DIPPING SAUCE

1/2 cup (4 fl oz/125 ml) rice vinegar

1 tablespoon sugar

1 tablespoon mirin

1 tablespoon soy sauce

1 lobster tail

1 nori sheet

1 cup (5 oz/150 g) prepared sushi rice
   (pages 20–21)

2 tablespoons katakuri starch or cornstarch
   (cornflour)

FOR TEMPURA

canola oil for deep-frying

a few drops Asian sesame oil

1 cup (8 fl oz/250 ml) cold water

1 cup (5 oz/150 g) tempura flour

2 chives, finely chopped

1 hard-boiled egg yolk, sieved (egg mimosa)

To make dipping sauce: Combine all ingredients in a bowl and mix well; set aside. Beginning on the softer underside of lobster, insert tip of a large knife and cut meat from shell, leaving meat in a whole piece. Transfer meat to a board and slice it in half, making sure not to cut all the way through and leaving 3/8 inch (1 cm) uncut, then open it to have 1 large flat slice of lobster. Trim meat to three-quarters of size of nori sheet.

Arrange nori sheet, glossy side down, on a sushi mat. Place lobster meat on nori and, with wet fingers, arrange sushi rice over lobster. Roll following instructions on pages 24–25. If nori is dry, wet edge and press mat to seal. Place katakuri starch in a flat plate and coat lobster roll. Allow roll to rest, seam side down, for 2 minutes.

Unroll mat and transfer roll to a cutting board. Wipe a sharp knife with a damp towel and cut roll into 4 even pieces, wiping knife after each cut.

Fill a tempura pan, or deep-fryer one-third full with canola oil and heat over medium-high heat to 365°F (185°C). Add a few drops of sesame oil.

Meanwhile, to make tempura batter, put tempura flour in a medium bowl and gradually whisk in cold water until mixture resembles a light pancake batter. Dip 2 rolls in batter and deep-fry, turning as necessary, until golden. Using a wire-mesh skimmer, transfer to a wire rack, or paper towels, to drain. Set aside on paper towels. Repeat with remaining rolls. Transfer rolls to serving plates and top with egg mimosa and chives. Serve with prepared dipping sauce.

Makes 4 pieces

Smoked salmon and asparagus with cream cheese

1 nori sheet

1 cup (5 oz/150 g) prepared sushi rice (pages 20–21)

1 teaspoon wasabi paste

2 tablespoons cream cheese

4 slices smoked salmon

4 asparagus spears, blanched and chilled

4 fresh dill sprigs, minced

soy sauce for serving

Cover a sushi mat with plastic wrap. Place nori on plastic, glossy side down, and, with wet fingers, spread sushi rice over nori, leaving uncovered a ³/₄-inch (2-cm) strip of nori on side farthest from you. Holding surface of rice with one hand, turn over rice and nori so that rice is on plastic and nori is on top. Return to mat. Using your index finger, smear wasabi and cream cheese over nori. Arrange 2 salmon slices and 2 asparagus spears in center, allowing asparagus to poke out of nori at both ends. Roll sushi following instructions on pages 24–25. Make sure fillings are enclosed but leave one-fourth of nori visible at end farthest from you. Lift up mat and roll forward to join nori edges. Press gently to form into a square shape.

Unroll mat, remove plastic, and transfer roll to a cutting board. Wipe a sharp knife with a damp cloth, cut roll in half, then cut each half into 4 pieces, wiping knife after each cut. Coat rolls with dill. Place rolls on plates and serve with soy sauce.

Makes 8 pieces

Shrimp tempura rolls with basil

FOR THAI BASIL SAUCE

1 tablespoon rice vinegar

1 teaspoon fish sauce

leaves from 2 Thai basil sprigs, finely chopped

1 teaspoon packed brown sugar

1 nori sheet, halved

2 cups (10 oz/300 g) prepared sushi rice
 (pages 20–21)

4 cooked shrimp tempura (page 34)

4 fresh Thai basil leaves

1 hard-boiled egg yolk, sieved (egg mimosa)

To make Thai basil sauce: Combine all ingredients in a bowl and mix well. Set aside.

Arrange one half sheet of nori, glossy side down, on a sushi mat. With wet fingers, spread half sushi rice evenly over nori, leaving uncovered a ¾-inch (2-cm) strip of nori on side farthest from you. Place 2 shrimp tempura over rice, allowing tails to poke out at both ends of nori. Top with 2 Thai basil leaves and roll following instructions on pages 24–25. If nori is too dry to seal, wet edge and press with mat.

Unroll mat, and transfer roll to a cutting board. Wipe a sharp knife with a damp towel and cut each roll into 4 pieces, wiping knife after each cut. Repeat with remaining ingredients. Arrange pieces on plates and sprinkle sieved egg yolk over shrimp tails. Serve with Thai basil sauce.

Makes 8 pieces

Rainbow rolls

3 arugula (rocket) leaves

3 beet (beetroot) leaves

1 slice cuttlefish or squid

1 slice salmon

1 slice king fish or yellowtail

1 cooked shrimp (prawn), about 2³/₄ inches (7 cm)
   long without head, shelled, halved and deveined

1 slice mango

1 cup (5 oz/150 g) prepared sushi rice
   (pages 20–21)

¹/₂ teaspoon wasabi paste

soy sauce for serving

Cover a sushi mat with plastic wrap. Begining from one edge of mat, line up arugula and beet leaves one after another, placing them on a slight diagonal, and leaving some space in between for cuttlefish, salmon, king fish, shrimp, and mango slices. Place fish and mango slices in between arugula and beet leaves.

With wet fingers, form sushi rice into a bar and place on top. Using your index finger, smear rice with a dab of wasabi. Lift up sushi mat and firmly roll sushi, following instructions on pages 24–25.

Unroll mat and transfer roll to a cutting board. Wipe a sharp knife with a damp towel, and cut roll in half. Cut each half into 3 pieces, wiping knife after each cut. Remove plastic and serve with soy sauce.

Makes 6 pieces

Tip

In Japan, this sushi is called **Tazuna-zushi,** *which means string-shaped hand rolls. The wrapping reveals the colorful ingredients and makes it more enticing to taste.*

Cooked shrimp are available from seafood markets. To cook shrimp, boil in an uncovered saucepan of salted water until they become firm and change color, 3–5 minutes. Remove and place in iced water until cool.

Dragon rolls

1 sheet nori, halved

2 cups (10 oz/300 g) prepared sushi rice
(pages 20–21)

1/2 English (hothouse) cucumber, halved
lengthwise, seeded, then cut into strips 1/4 inch
(6 mm) thick

1/2 fillet barbecued eel, cut into strips

1 avocado, halved, pitted and peeled

4 teaspoons umeboshi (pickled plum) puree

soy sauce for serving

Cover a sushi mat with plastic wrap. Place a half sheet of nori on plastic, glossy side down, and, with wet fingers, spread half sushi rice evenly over nori. Holding surface of rice with one hand, turn over rice and nori so rice is on plastic and nori is on top. Arrange cucumber and eel strips in center of nori. Using sushi mat, roll to enclose fillings, leaving a 3/4-inch (2-cm) strip of nori visible at end farthest from you. Lift up sushi mat and roll following instructions on pages 24–25. Press gently to firm shape and seal nori.

Unroll mat, remove plastic, and transfer roll to a cutting board. Wipe a sharp knife with a damp towel and cut roll in half. Repeat with remaining ingredients.

With a small sharp knife, slice an avocado half thinly, keeping slices together, and place it over a sushi roll, pushing gently with your fingers to curve avocado slices. Repeat with other avocado half. Arrange rolls on serving plates and top each piece with 3 drops umeboshi puree. Serve with soy sauce. Eat with a knife and fork.

Makes 4 pieces

Tips

Barbecued eel is sold in airtight bags from Japanese and other Asian markets, and some fish stores. Umeboshi (pickled plum) puree is sold in tubes and bottles in Japanese markets.

Roast pork and scallion rolls

1/2 sheet nori

1 cup (5 oz/150 g) prepared sushi rice
   (pages 20–21)

2 strips roast pork, each 3/8 inch (1 cm) wide and
   8 inches (20 cm) long

2 scallions (shallots/spring onions), trimmed

sweet and sour chili sauce for serving (available
   from Asian markets)

Place nori on a sushi mat, glossy side down. With wet fingers, spread rice evenly over nori. Place pork strips and scallions in center of nori and roll following instructions on pages 24–25. Unroll mat and transfer roll to a cutting board. Wipe a sharp knife with a damp towel and cut roll in half, then cut each half in half again, wiping knife after each cut. Serve with chili sauce.

Makes 4 pieces

Cheese and parsley rolls

1/2 sheet nori

1 cup (5 oz/150 g) prepared sushi rice
   (pages 20–21)

1 teaspoon wasabi paste

2 sticks cheddar cheese, about 4 inches (10 cm)
   long

leaves from 2 sprigs parsley, chopped

soy sauce for serving

Place nori on a sushi mat, glossy side down, and, with wet fingers, spread rice evenly over nori. Using your index finger, smear center of rice with wasabi. Place cheese sticks end to end in a line in center of rice and cut off excess. Sprinkle with parsley, then firmly roll, following instructions on pages 24–25. Unroll mat and transfer roll to a cutting board. Wipe a sharp knife with a damp cloth and cut roll into 3 equal portions. Cut 2 portions in half, then cut third portion in half diagonally, wiping knife after each cut. Serve with soy sauce.

Makes 6 pieces

Vietnamese rice paper rolls with black rice

12 small cooked shrimp (prawns), shelled

4 square rice paper sheets

1 cup (5 oz/150 g) prepared black sushi rice
   (page 22)

1 teaspoon wasabi paste

2 tablespoons peanuts, crushed

4 cilantro (fresh coriander) sprigs, stemmed

8 fresh chives

sweet and sour chili sauce for serving

Cut shrimp in half from head to tail and remove vein. Soak 1 rice paper sheet at a time in a shallow bowl of warm water for 10 seconds. Drain, pat dry with paper towels, and transfer rice paper to a work surface.

Spread a quarter of rice across center of a rice paper sheet, leaving a 3/4-inch (2-cm) gap at each end of paper.

Dab a little wasabi on rice and sprinkle 1/2 tablespoon crushed peanuts over top. Layer a cilantro sprig and 4 shrimp halves in a line, cut side down, and top with 2 chives. Roll up rice paper to enclose fillings, tucking in one end and leaving other end open, with chives protruding. Repeat with remaining ingredients. Serve rolls immediately with sweet and sour chili sauce.

Makes 4 rolls

Tip

Sweet and sour chili sauce is available from supermarkets and Asian markets.

Cooked shrimp are available from seafood markets. To cook shrimp, boil in an uncovered saucepan of salted water until they become firm and change color, 3–5 minutes. Remove and place in iced water until cool.

VIETNAMESE RICE PAPER ROLLS WITH BLACK RICE

Broccoli and bell pepper cones

3 oz (100 g) broccoli, blanched in salted water for
  1 minute and drained

1/2 red bell pepper (capsicum), seeded

1 1/2 oz (45 g) cold Brie or Camembert cheese

1 cup (5 oz/150 g) prepared sushi rice
  (pages 20–21)

2 sheets nori, halved

1 teaspoon wasabi paste

2 tablespoons Japanese mayonnaise

Rinse broccoli under running water until chilled. Drain and pat with paper towels. Cut bell pepper lengthwise into pieces 1/4 inch (6 mm) thick. Slice cheese thinly. Holding a nori sheet half in your left hand, spread one-fourth of rice over almost half of nori and smear wasabi in center. Layer rice with cheese slices, broccoli, and bell pepper. Roll tightly into a cone roll, following instructions on pages 26–27. Repeat with remaining ingredients to make 3 more pieces. Top each piece with 1/2 tablespoon Japanese mayonnaise.

Makes 4 pieces

Small rolls with celery, pastrami, and pâté

1/2 sheet nori

1 cup (5 oz/150 g) prepared sushi rice (pages 20–21)

1 teaspoon chicken liver pâté

1/2 teaspoon chili paste

1 slice pastrami

1/2 celery stick, trimmed and thinly sliced
  lengthwise

soy sauce for serving

Place nori on a sushi mat, glossy side down. With wet hands, spread rice over nori. With your index finger, smear pâté and chili paste in a line down center of rice. Top with pastrami and celery. Roll tightly following instructions on pages 24–25. Unroll mat and transfer roll to a cutting board. Wipe a sharp knife with a damp towel. Cut roll in half, and cut both rolls in half again; then cut rolls again to make a total of 8 pieces, wiping knife after each cut. Serve with soy sauce.

Makes 8 pieces

Korean kimchi rolls

1 teaspoon canola oil

3 oz (90 g) topside steak, thinly sliced

2 tablespoons Korean barbecue sauce

1 cup (5 oz/150 g) prepared sushi rice
(pages 20–21)

2 Chinese (napa) cabbage kimchi leaves

2 fresh chives

2 tablespoons white sesame seeds

Heat a heavy frying pan over high heat and add oil. Reduce heat to medium, add steak slices and cook until heated through. Add barbecue sauce and cook for 1 minute. Set aside on a plate until cool.

Cover a sushi mat with plastic wrap. Lay kimchi leaves horizontally on plastic, beginning at end closest to you. With wet fingers, spread the rice over kimchi, leaving uncovered a 3/4-inch (2-cm) strip at end farthest from you. Cover with beef and arrange chives in center. Roll up tightly following instructions on pages 24–25.

Unroll mat, remove plastic, and transfer roll to a cutting board. Wipe a sharp knife with a damp towel and cut each roll in half, then cut each half in half again, wiping knife after each cut. Repeat with remaining ingredients.

Holding each piece with your fingers, dip into sesame seeds on a plate to coat kimchi. Arrange pieces on serving plates and serve.

Make 8 pieces

Tip

Korean barbecue sauce and kimchi are available from Japanese and Korean markets.

Indonesian-flavored coconut rolls

1 cup (5 oz/150 g) prepared sushi rice
  (pages 20–21)
1 tablespoon sate sauce
1 can coconut meat, drained
1 sheet nori, halved
chili (sambal) paste for serving

Cover a sushi mat with plastic wrap. Place a half sheet of nori over plastic, glossy side down, and, with wet fingers, spread half of sushi rice over nori. Holding surface of rice with one hand, turn over rice and nori, placing rice on plastic. Using your index finger, smear nori with sate sauce. Place 4 pieces coconut meat in center. Roll tightly, following instructions on pages 24–25.

Unroll mat, remove plastic, and transfer roll to a cutting board. Wipe a sharp knife with a damp towel and cut roll in half; then cut each half into 3 pieces, wiping knife after each cut. Repeat with remaining ingredients. Serve with chili paste.

Makes 12 pieces

Tip

Unshredded preserved coconut meat is sold in tins or bottles. This milky-colored coconut meat has a light, fruity taste. Available from large supermarkets or Asian markets.

Thai-flavored papaya and vegetable rolls

¹/₄ English (hothouse) cucumber, seeded and
  julienned

¹/₄ carrot, peeled and julienned

¹/₄ papaya (cut lengthwise), peeled and seeded

³/₄ sheet nori

1 cup (5 oz/150 g) prepared sushi rice (pages 20–21)

2 fresh Thai basil leaves

2 tablespoons green curry paste

Cut cucumber into strips, each ¹/₄ inch (6 mm) thick. Cut carrot and papaya into strips the same size. Set aside on a plate.

Cover a sushi mat with plastic wrap. Place nori over plastic, glossy side down, and, with wet fingers, spread sushi rice over nori. Holding surface of rice with one hand, turn over rice and nori, placing rice on plastic. Arrange cucumber, carrot, and papaya strips and basil leaves in center. Roll tightly, following instructions on pages 24–25.

Unroll mat, remove plastic, and transfer roll to a cutting board. Wipe a sharp knife with a damp towel and cut roll in half. Cut rolls in half, then cut each piece again, wiping knife after each cut.

Arrange pieces on plates and spoon curry paste alongside.

Makes 8 pieces

THAI-FLAVORED PAPAYA AND VEGETABLE ROLLS

Pink rice rolls with chili jam

2 cups (14 oz/440 g) raw sushi rice or
short-grain rice

2 cups (16 fl oz/500 ml) beet (beetroot) juice in
place of water

FOR CHILI-JAM SAUCE

2 tablespoons strawberry jam

1 teaspoon chili paste

2 tablespoons rice vinegar

1 teaspoon chili paste

1 tablespoon Japanese mayonnaise

4 round rice paper sheets

2 scallions (shallots/spring onions), quartered
lengthwise

Prepare sushi rice following the instructions on pages 20–21, but substitute beet juice for cooking water. This creates the "pink" color of the rice.

To make chili-jam sauce: Mix together all the ingredients in a small bowl, and set aside.

In another small bowl, mix chili paste and Japanese mayonnaise. Set aside.

Divide pink sushi rice into 4 equal portions and shape into 4 balls.

Soak 1 rice paper sheet at a time, for 10 seconds, in a shallow dish of warm water. Drain and pat dry with paper towels. Transfer to a clean work surface. Place a pink sushi rice ball in center of a sheet of rice paper and, using a spoon, spread chili mayonnaise on top. Wrap like a parcel, folding in the top and bottom, then rolling up. Then wrap 1 strip of scallion around each roll and tie with a knot. Serve with chili-jam sauce.

Makes 4 pieces

Black rice rolls with apricot glacé

FOR APRICOT GLACÉ

12 dried apricots

¹/₂ cup (4 fl oz/125 ml) water

¹/₄ cup (2 oz/60 g) sugar

1 teaspoon Grand Marnier liqueur

1 teaspoon sake (Japanese rice wine)

1 sheet nori, halved

1 cup (5 oz/150 g) prepared black sushi rice
(page 22)

¹/₂ teaspoon chili paste

To make apricot glacé: Combine apricots and water in a saucepan and bring to a boil over high heat. Reduce heat to low, add sugar, and cook for 10 minutes. Add Grand Marnier and sake and cook, stirring occasionally, until most of the liquid has been absorbed. Remove from heat and set aside to cool.

Cover a sushi mat with plastic wrap. Place a nori half sheet on plastic, glossy side down, and, with wet fingers, spread half the black sushi rice all over nori. Holding surface of rice with one hand, turn over rice and nori, placing rice on the plastic. Using your index finger, smear half chili paste over nori and arrange 6 cooked apricots in center.

Using a sushi mat, roll following instructions on pages 24–25, enclosing fillings and leaving one-fourth of nori uncovered at end farthest from you. Lift up mat and roll forward to join nori edges. Press gently to firm shape.

Unroll mat, remove plastic, and transfer roll to a cutting board. Wipe a sharp knife with a damp towel and cut roll in half; then cut each piece into 3, wiping knife after each cut. Repeat with remaining ingredients.

Arrange sushi on plates and serve.

Makes 12 pieces

Triangle rolls with dried mango and jumbo shrimp

1 sheet nori

12 slices dried mango

1 cup (5 oz/150 g) prepared sushi rice
(pages 20–21)

1 teaspoon red horseradish sauce

3 cooked jumbo shrimp (prawns), shelled and
deveined

soy sauce for serving

Place nori sheet on a sushi mat, glossy side down. Place dried mango slices in rows over three-fourths of nori and, with wet fingers, spread sushi rice over mango. Spread red horseradish sauce across center and top with shrimp.

Roll tightly, following the instructions on pages 24–25, but, while rolling, use pressure from your fingers to form roll into a triangular shape.

Unroll mat and transfer roll to a cutting board. Wipe a sharp knife with a damp towel and cut roll in half; then cut each piece into 4, wiping knife after each cut. Arrange pieces on serving plates. Serve with soy sauce.

Make 8 pieces

Tip

Cooked shrimp are available from seafood markets. To cook shrimp, boil in an uncovered saucepan of salted water until they become firm and change color, 3–5 minutes. Remove and place in iced water until cool.

nigiri-zushi

Step-by-step nigiri-zushi

1. Cut salmon slices into strips ¼ inch (6 mm) thick, ¾ inch (2 cm) wide, and 2 inches (5 cm) long. Hold salmon slice with left hand. Wet right hand and shape a portion of rice into a finger about ¼ inch (6 mm) thick, ¾ inch (2 cm) wide, and 2 inches (5 cm) long. With tip of right index finger, dab wasabi on salmon slice.

2. Using your index finger, press rice onto the wasabi-dabbed salmon slice.

3. Turn rice and salmon over so that salmon is on top. Using your index and middle fingers, mold salmon around rice so that there is no rice showing around the edges.

4. With right fingers, turn molded salmon and rice 180 degrees and repeat molding. Serve with soy sauce. To eat, dip the salmon, not the rice, into the soy sauce.

Soy nigiri with melted cheese

2 cups (10 oz/300 g) prepared sushi rice
(pages 20–21)

1 piece salmon, about 6¹/₂–7³/₄ oz (200–240 g),
cut into 8 slices, ¹/₄ inch (6 mm) thick, 1¹/₄
inches (3 cm) wide, and 2¹/₂ inches (6 cm) long

8 teaspoons soy sauce

4 slices cheese, halved

8 kinome (prickly ash) or parsley sprigs

Preheat broiler (grill) to medium heat. Line a small baking sheet with aluminum foil. Meanwhile, take one-eighth of rice and shape it into a finger about ¼ inch (6 mm) thick, ¾ inch (2 cm) wide, and 2 inches (5 cm) long. Mold rice and salmon together following instructions on page 64, making sure they are firmly molded, and place on a plate. Repeat with remaining salmon and rice. Pour soy sauce over sushi.

Transfer sushi to baking sheet and place under broiler (grill) as close as possible to the heating element. Broil (grill), turning once, until browned on each side.

Top each sushi with a half cheese slice. Return to broiler (grill) and broil (grill) until cheese has melted. Arrange a sprig of kinome on top of each piece and serve immediately.

Makes 8 pieces

Tip

If you would like to have wasabi with this sushi, put wasabi on the sushi before placing cheese on top.

Blueberry sushi with honey chili

1 English (hothouse) cucumber

1 cup (5 oz/150g) prepared sushi rice
  (pages 20–21)

4 tablespoons (1 oz/30 g) blueberries

2 fresh small red chili peppers, halved, seeded,
  and cut into fine julienne

FOR HONEY-CHILI SAUCE

1 fresh chili, seeded and finely chopped

2 tablespoons honey

Using a vegetable peeler, peel off a wide, lengthwise slice of cucumber skin and discard. Place cucumber on a cutting board, cut side up, hold firmly, and with the peeler, peel a paper-thin slice about $1\frac{1}{2}$ inches (4 cm) wide and 4 inches (10 cm) long. (The strip will have a narrow green outer edge of skin and white flesh in the center. The skin allows the cucumber to stick to the rice.) Repeat to make 3 more slices.

With wet hands, shape rice into 4 fingers following instructions on page 64. Wrap a cucumber strip around outside of each rice finger. Top with 1 tablespoon blueberries and 1 chili strip. Place sushi rolls on a plate.

To make honey-chili sauce: Mix chili and honey together in a bowl.

Pour sauce over sushi rolls to serve.

Makes 4 pieces

Sun-dried tomato and anchovy

1 scallion (shallot/spring onion)

4 oil-packed sun-dried tomatoes, drained

2 tablespoons black sesame seeds

1 cup (5 oz/150g) prepared sushi rice
  (pages 20–21)

wasabi paste to taste

4 anchovies, drained

soy sauce for serving

Cut scallion in half lengthwise, then cut into 4 thin strips. Place in a bowl of cold water until slices curl, then drain. Place sun-dried tomatoes on a cutting board and cut almost through horizontally, then open tomato like a butterfly.

Place sesame seeds on a plate.

With wet hands, shape rice into 4 fingers, following instructions on page 64. Top each piece with wasabi, 1 sun-dried tomato, and 1 anchovy. Place sushi, rice side down, onto sesame seeds to coat rice. Arrange sushi on a plate and garnish with scallion curls.

Serve with soy sauce.

Makes 4 pieces

BLUEBERRY SUSHI WITH HONEY CHILI

Mango and kimchi nigiri

1 mango, peeled and cut from pit

2 cups (10 oz/300 g) prepared sushi rice
   (pages 20–21)

8 pieces Chinese (napa) cabbage kimchi

1 nori sheet, cut into 8 strips, each 3/8 inch (1 cm)
   wide and 4 inches (10 cm) long

Cut mango flesh into 8 strips, each about 1¼ inches (3 cm) thick. Shape rice into 8 fingers, following instructions on page 64. Top each rice finger with a mango strip and a piece of kimchi. Tie a nori strip around sushi like a belt, place on serving plates, and serve.

Makes 8 pieces

Salmon and liver pâté sushi with sesame seeds

1 scallion (shallot/spring onion), trimmed

1 cup (5 oz/150 g) prepared sushi rice
   (pages 20–21)

2 tablespoons white sesame seeds, toasted

4 salmon or 4 liver pâté slices, each 1¼ inches
   (3 cm) wide, 2½ inches (6 cm) long and ¼ inch
   (6 mm) thick

4 aspic slices (from top of salmon pâté) or 4 aspic
   slices (from top of liver pâté)

wasabi paste to taste

Cut scallion in half lengthwise, then slice again to make 4 thin strips. Put in a bowl of cold water until slices curl. Drain, pat dry with paper towels, and set aside. With wet hands, mold rice into 4 fingers, following instructions on page 64. Place white sesame seeds on a plate and dip one side of each rice finger into seeds, pressing gently to seal seeds onto sushi. Top with a pâté slice, then place scallion on the pâté. Top with an aspic slice.

Serve with wasabi paste. Since pâté is quite rich in flavor, you do not need soy sauce.

Makes 4 pieces

MANGO AND KIMCHI NIGIRI

Grilled chicken ships

2¹/₄ sheets nori

1 teaspoon canola oil

1 skinless, boneless chicken breast, about

  7 oz (220 g)

2 cups (10 oz/300 g) prepared sushi rice

  (pages 20–21)

4 tablespoons (2 oz/60 g) Japanese mayonnaise

8 small curly endive (curly chicory) leaves

2 tablespoons umeboshi (pickled plum) puree

Using cooking scissors, cut ¼ sheet of nori into very thin strips. Set aside on a plate.

Also using scissors, cut 2 nori sheets into quarters. Set aside on a dry work surface.

Heat a grill pan over medium-high heat and add oil. Add chicken, reduce heat to medium, and cook until cooked through, about 10 minutes. Transfer chicken to a plate and let cool slightly. With your fingers, shred chicken into fine strips. Transfer to a medium bowl, add mayonnaise and stir well.

With wet hands, mold rice into 8 fingers, following the instructions on page 64.

With dry fingers of one hand, pick up a piece of nori and wrap it around rice (rough side in), sealing on one end and leaving other end open like a pouch. Press shredded chicken onto rice through open nori end. Insert a curly endive leaf and sprinkle with thin nori strips. Repeat with remaining ingredients. Serve with umeboshi puree.

Makes 8 pieces

Tips

This type of sushi has a wide belt of nori wrapped around the sushi rice supporting a loose topping such as caviar, shredded chicken, or sea urchin roe. Because of its shape, this sushi is known as gunkan, which means "black ship" or "warrior" ship.

Umeboshi (pickled plum) puree is sold in tubes or small bottles at Japanese or other Asian markets.

Tandoori chicken-daikon ships

1 small boneless, skinless chicken breast, about
  5¹/₂ oz (170 g)
¹/₄ cup (2 fl oz/60 ml) tandoori paste
1 large daikon, halved and peeled
1 teaspoon canola oil
2 cups (10 oz/300 g) prepared sushi rice
  (pages 20–21)
2 tablespoons plain (natural) yogurt
8 caperberries

FOR VINAIGRETTE
2 teaspoons soy sauce
1 tablespoon mirin
1 tablespoon rice vinegar

Spread tandoori paste on both sides of chicken and let chicken sit for 20 minutes. Place a daikon half on a cutting board, cut side up, and, holding daikon steady with your hand, use a vegetable peeler to cut 8 long, thin, wide slices. Place slices in a bowl of water and set aside.

Heat a frying pan over medium-high heat and add oil. Add marinated chicken to pan and cook, on both sides, until cooked through. Transfer chicken to a cutting board, let cool slightly, then cut lengthwise into 8 thin slices.

Drain daikon slices and pat dry with paper towels.

With wet hands, mold sushi rice into 8 fingers, following the instructions on page 64. Holding rice with one hand, pick up a daikon slice and wrap it around rice, pressing gently to make sure it sticks to rice. Top with a dollop of yogurt and a chicken slice. Repeat with remaining ingredients. Top each sushi with a caperberry.

To make vinaigrette: Combine all ingredients in a bowl and stir to mix. Divide among individual sauce dishes and serve alongside sushi for dipping.

Makes 8 pieces

Tip

Tandoori paste is available from supermarkets and Indian or other Asian markets.

sushi

Triangle sushi with tobikko, wasabi and daikon

1 daikon, peeled

1 cup (5 oz/150 g) prepared sushi rice
    (pages 20–21)

4 tablespoons (1¼ oz/40 g) wasabi tobikko

1 tablespoon wasabi paste

nandina leaves or small camellia leaves for
    garnish

soy sauce for serving

Using a vegetable peeler, cut daikon lengthwise into 4 long, thin, wide slices. Place them in a bowl of water and set aside.

Place a triangle mold, with a base 2 inches (5 cm) wide, on a cutting board and place a piece of plastic wrap loosely inside mold. Using a wet rice paddle, put one-fourth of sushi rice in mold and press to shape. Carefully remove mold, invert onto a work surface, and, holding rice with one hand, peel off plastic wrap. Repeat with remaining ingredients to make 3 more sushi. Spread 1 tablespoon tobikko evenly over each.

Drain daikon slices and pat dry with paper towels. Using your index finger, spread a small amount of wasabi over center of each daikon slice. Wrap a daikon slice, wasabi side in, around the bottom of a sushi. Repeat with remaining daikon slices. Transfer each sushi onto an individual plate. Insert a nandina leaf in the center of each for garnish, and serve with soy sauce. Eat with a knife and fork.

Makes 4 pieces

TRIANGLE SUSHI WITH TOBIKKO. WASABI AND DAIKON

Heart sushi with aonori paste and gold leaf

2 cups (10 oz/300 g) prepared sushi rice
 (pages 20–21)
1 teaspoon wasabi paste
1 hard-boiled egg yolk, sieved (egg mimosa)
1 snapper fillet, about 5¹/₂ oz (170 g), cut into
 4 pieces
8 teaspoons aonori paste
1 sheet edible gold leaf

Immerse a small heart-shaped mold, such as a cookie cutter, in a bowl of water. Transfer it to a work surface. Using a wet teaspoon or chopsticks, put sushi rice in mold, leaving a quarter of the mold empty. Holding mold with one hand and pushing top of rice with other hand, carefully remove mold from the formed rice. (Alternatively, use plastic wrap as for triangle sushi, page 72). Repeat with remaining rice to make four pieces.

Smear a small amount of wasabi thinly over rice and top with one-fourth of egg mimosa and a piece of fish. Spread 2 teaspoons aonori paste over fish and top with a piece of gold leaf. Repeat with remaining ingredients to make 3 more pieces.

Place heart sushi on serving plates and serve. Eat with chopsticks or a knife and fork.

Makes 4 pieces

Tip

Edible gold leaf is available from stores that sell cake decorations. It is also added to sake (Japanese rice wine) on special occasions.

HEART SUSHI WITH AONORI PASTE AND GOLD LEAF

Square sushi with tuna and edible flowers

7 oz (200 g) fresh tuna block

2 cups (10 oz/300 g) prepared sushi rice
  (pages 20–21)

8 fresh chives

4 edible flowers, such as violas or nasturtiums

3/4 x 2-inch (2 x 5-cm) piece ginger, peeled and
  grated

wasabi paste for serving

soy sauce for serving

Trim the tuna block to a 2¹/2-inch (6-cm) square that is 3 inches (7 cm) thick.

Boil water and pour into a heatproof, nonmetallic bowl. Immerse tuna block in boiling water for a few seconds to blanch the outer surface. Transfer to clean kitchen towels and pat dry.

Place tuna block on a cutting board. Using a large, sharp knife, cut tuna block horizontally into 4 squares, each 3/4 inch (2 cm) thick.

Place a piece of plastic wrap on a work surface. Wet a 2¹/2-inch (6-cm) square mold and place on plastic wrap. Using a rice paddle, put one-fourth of sushi rice in mold and press to form. With wet hands, remove the mold and plastic wrap, pushing over the rice with one hand. Place a tuna square on molded rice and top with an edible flower or serve on the plate. Repeat with remaining ingredients to make 3 more pieces.

Tie 2 chives around each rice square. Serve with grated ginger, wasabi, and soy sauce on the plate. Eat with a knife and fork.

Makes 4 pieces

Tip

Packets of edible flowers are sold in some specialty foods stores.

Mille-feuille sushi with blue cheese and pastrami

1 scallion (shallot/spring onion)

6 oz (185 g) pastrami slices

1 teaspoon wasabi paste

4 tablespoons Japanese mayonnaise

2 cups (10 oz/300 g) prepared sushi rice
   (pages 20–21)

4 tablespoons (1 oz/30 g) blue cheese

1 tablespoon pine nuts

4 nori strips, each 3/8 inch (1 cm) wide and
   4 inches (10 cm) long

8 beet (beetroot) leaves

Cut scallion in half lengthwise, then cut each piece in half again to make 4 strips. Place in a bowl of cold water to let curls form.

Place a small hexagonal mold on each slice of pastrami in turn, then cut around the mold with a small knife to make 8 hexagonal pastrami shapes.

Combine wasabi paste and Japanese mayonnaise in a small bowl. Stir to blend.

Cut a piece of plastic wrap about 6 inches (15 cm) long and place loosely inside mold. Place 1/4 cup (1 oz/30 g) sushi rice in mold and press down with a wet rice paddle. Spread 1 tablespoon blue cheese over sushi rice and lay a pastrami shape on top. Add another 1/4 cup (1 oz/30 g) sushi rice and top with another piece pastrami. Holding plastic wrap, remove sushi from mold and transfer to individual plates. Spread wasabi mixture over pastrami and top with a pinch of pine nuts and a small curl of scallion. Repeat with remaining ingredients to make 3 more sushi.

Wrap a nori strip around the bottom of each sushi. Arrange with 2 beetroot leaves.

Makes 4 pieces

MILLE-FEUILLE SUSHI WITH BLUE CHEESE AND PASTRAMI

hand rolls

Vegetarian cone rolls with balsamic vinegar

1 carrot, peeled

1 daikon, peeled

2 cups (10 oz/300 g) prepared sushi rice
(pages 20–21)

1/2 teaspoon wasabi paste

8 small beet (beetroot) leaves

12 kaiware (radish sprouts) or mustard cress
sprouts

12 enoki mushrooms with stems

balsamic vinegar for dipping

Using a vegetable peeler, cut 4 long, thin, wide strips from carrot, and 4 from daikon. With a wet hand, spread rice on the strips in a triangular shape. Using your index finger, smear wasabi in a line down the center, and place 2 beet leaves, kaiware, and enoki mushrooms over wasabi. Roll up to form a cone, gently pushing in the ingredients. Wrap cone in a 4 x 8-inch (10 x 20-cm) rectangle of cellophane to hold it closed. Repeat with remaining ingredients to make 3 more cones.

Serve with balsamic vinegar.

Makes 4 cones

Tip

Kaiware are available in Japanese markets.

VEGETARIAN CONE ROLLS WITH BALSAMIC VINEGAR

Ruby grapefruit and apple mint cone rolls

1 ruby grapefruit (pink grapefruit)

2 cups (10 oz/300 g) prepared sushi rice
  (pages 20–21)

4 sprigs apple mint or other mint

2 sheets nori, halved

FOR HONEY CHILI

1 red chili, seeded and thinly sliced

4 teaspoons honey

To prepare grapefruit, cut off ends of grapefruit down to the flesh. Place on one end on a cutting board. Using a small, sharp knife, cut off peel vertically down to the flesh. Holding grapefruit over a bowl, cut on either side of membrane to release segments into the bowl.

Using one-fourth of the grapefruit segments, and spreading sushi rice on rough side of nori, make a cone roll following instructions on pages 26–27. Wrap cone in a 4 x 8-inch (10 x 20-cm) rectangle of cellophane to keep fresh. Insert a mint sprig in the top. Repeat with remaining ingredients to make 3 more rolls.

To make honey chili: Stir together chili and honey in a small bowl. Drizzle over sushi, and serve.

Makes 4 cones

Prosciutto and baby spinach cone rolls

2 cups (10 oz/300 g) prepared sushi rice
(pages 20–21)

2 nori sheets, halved

1 teaspoon wasabi paste

8 baby spinach leaves

4 prosciutto slices

4 teaspoons Japanese mayonnaise

4 capers

Following the instructions on pages 26–27, spread sushi rice on rough side of one piece of nori. Smear wasabi in a line down center of rice. Place 2 baby spinach leaves and 1 slice proscuitto on top. Roll up to form a cone. Top cone with 1 teaspoon Japanese mayonnaise and a caper. Repeat with remaining ingredients to make 3 more cones.

Serve with soy sauce.

Makes 4 cones

Green tea soba and pistachio

3¹/₂ oz (100 g) green tea soba noodles (available
   in Japanese and Asian markets)

2 sheets nori, quartered

1 teaspoon green Tabasco sauce

4 tablespoons (³/₄ oz/20 g) smooth peanut butter

2 tablespoons pistachio nuts, crushed

SOY VINAIGRETTE

1 teaspoon mirin

2 tablespoons rice vinegar

1 tablespoon soy sauce

In a large pot of salted, boiling water, cook soba noodles until just tender, following instructions on package. Drain noodles in a strainer and rinse under running water, occasionally turning the noodles with your hand, until cold. Drain well.

With dry hands, place 1 nori piece on a dry work surface. Place one-eighth of soba noodles on nori and sprinkle with green Tabasco sauce.

Roll following the instructions on pages 26–27, then form into a wedge shape. Gently but firmly press the end to seal. Spread with ¹/₂ tablespoon peanut butter. Sprinkle with pistachio nuts. Repeat with remaining ingredients to make 7 more pieces. Arrange 2 pieces on each plate.

To make soy vinaigrette: Combine mirin, vinegar and soy sauce in a bowl and stir. Serve vinaigrette in individual bowls.

Eat with fingers or chopsticks.

Makes 8 pieces

Salami and daikon sushi

1 crosswise slice daikon, ³/₈ inch (1 cm) thick

1 nori sheet, cut into quarters

1 cup (5 oz/150 g) prepared sushi rice (pages 20–21)

2 twiggy salami sticks, each cut into 4 sticks
   lengthwise, 4 inches (10 cm) long and ¹/₄ inch
   (6 mm) thick

1 teaspoon tobikko

Using a flower-shaped vegetable cutter, stamp a flower shape into daikon piece. Using a sharp knife, cut flower into 4 horizontal slices. Put slices in a bowl of water with a splash of rice vinegar added.

Put nori quarters on a dry work surface. With wet fingers, spread sushi rice over half of each quarter. Arrange 2 salami slices in center of rice and roll up tightly. Place roll upright in a small glass. Drain daikon flowers and pat dry with paper towels. With a toothpick, pierce a daikon flower and top with a dot of tobikko in center, then insert into sushi. Repeat to garnish remaining sushi.

Makes 4 pieces

GREEN TEA SOBA AND PISTACHIO

hand-rolled sushi

Mango chutney and turnip chirashi-zushi

8 baby turnips

2 cups (10 oz/300 g) prepared sushi rice
(pages 20–21)

4 teaspoons vindaloo paste

8 teaspoons mango chutney

8 fresh raspberries

8 mango spears, each 3/8 inch (1 cm) wide,
and 1 inch (2.5 cm) long

Trim tops of turnips, leaving 3/8 inch (1 cm) of stem intact, and set aside. Using a small, sharp knife, cut a slice from bottom of each turnip so that they sit upright, then pare the sides to form a hexagonal shape.

Using a teaspoon, scoop out the inside of each turnip, leaving a thin shell. Or cut an 1/8-inch (3-mm) thick slice from top of each turnip and reserve.

In a pot of salted boiling water, cook turnips and reserved tops until tender, about 10 minutes. Transfer to iced water and let cool. Drain upside down on paper towels and pat dry.

Fill each turnip with mango chutney and sushi rice. Spread 1/2 teaspoon vindaloo paste over rice and top with a raspberry. Insert 1 mango slice into rice. Arrange sushi on a plate with a turnip top leaning against the side of each. Eat with fingers.

Makes 8 pieces

Tip

If fresh mango is unavailable, use canned mango. Vindaloo paste is an Indian curry paste, similar to madras curry. Purchase in jars or cans from supermarkets and store in the refrigerator after opening.

MANGO CHUTNEY AND TURNIP CHIRASHI-ZUSHI

Saffron rice and lettuce chirashi-zushi

FOR SAFFRON SUSHI RICE

1 teaspoon saffron

1 cup (7 oz/220 g) raw sushi rice

1 cup (8 fl oz/250 ml) water

1/4 cup (2 fl oz/60 ml) rice vinegar

2 tablespoons sugar

pinch of salt

FOR STRAWBERRY JAM VINAIGRETTE

1/4 cup (2 1/2 oz/75 g) strawberry jam

1/4 cup (2 fl oz/60 ml) rice vinegar

1 1/2 oz (40 g) preserved herring roe, chopped

4 fresh chives, finely chopped

4 iceberg lettuce leaves

strawberry leaves for garnish

To make saffron sushi rice: Follow the instructions on pages 20–21, adding saffron to cooling water and mixing cooked rice with vinegar, sugar, and salt. Let cool to room temperature.

To make strawberry vinaigrette: Mix together strawberry jam and rice vinegar in a small bowl.

Add herring roe, and chives to the vinaigrette. Stir to blend together.

Place a lettuce leaf on each of 4 serving plates. Into each leaf, spoon one-fourth of sushi rice to one side. Then spoon one-fourth of herring roe mixture alongside sushi rice. Insert a strawberry leaf as garnish.

Eat sushi with chopsticks, or a knife and a fork.

Tip

Preserved herring roe is available from Japanese markets. Tobikko may be substituted.

Ground meat and eggplant chirashi-zushi

FOR ONION VINAIGRETTE

1/4 onion, finely chopped

2 tablespoons rice vinegar

1 teaspoon olive oil

1 teaspoon sugar

1 tablespoon soy sauce

4 purple baby eggplants (aubergines), about 2
   inches (5 cm) in diameter

canola oil for deep-frying

3 oz (90 g) ground (minced) lean beef, stir-fried
   until color has changed

2 cups (10 oz/300 g) prepared sushi rice
   (pages 20–21)

1 teaspoon grated fresh ginger

1 teaspoon wasabi paste

4 quail eggs

4 teaspoons mustard cress

T o make onion vinaigrette: Whisk together all ingredients in a bowl until well combined. Set aside.

Place an eggplant on its side on a cutting board. Using a sharp knife, cut off a lengthwise slice of eggplant about 3/8 inch (1 cm) thick. Using a teaspoon, scoop out inside of eggplant, leaving stem intact and making a shell about 3/8 inch (1 cm) thick. Reserve eggplant flesh for another use.

Fill a tempura pan, or deep-fryer one-third full with canola oil and heat over medium-high heat to 365°F (185°C). Deep-fry each eggplant shell separately, occasionally stirring with chopsticks, until soft. Drain eggplant, upside down, on wire rack in tempura pan, or in a wire-mesh skimmer, for 30 seconds. Transfer to paper towels. Repeat with remaining eggplants.

In a medium bowl, combine meat, sushi rice, ginger, and wasabi paste. Stir to blend, then spoon into each eggplant. Carefully separate quail eggs, making sure not to break the yolk. Gently slip 1 yolk on top of each eggplant and garnish with mustard cress. Arrange each eggplant on a plate and pour onion vinaigrette around it.

Makes 4 pieces

GROUND MEAT AND EGGPLANT CHIRASHI-ZUSHI

Parmesan cheese chirashi-zushi in tomato

1/2 English (hothouse) cucumber

4 vine-ripened tomatoes

2 cups (10 oz/300 g) prepared sushi rice
  (pages 20–21)

8 Parmesan cheese shavings, plus
  1/4 cup (1 oz/30 g) grated Parmesan

2 egg yolks

FOR OLIVE OIL VINAIGRETTE

2 tablespoons rice vinegar

1 tablespoon sugar

pinch of salt

2 teaspoons olive oil

leaves from 4 parsley sprigs, finely chopped

Cut cucumber into lengthwise slices, then cut the slices crosswise in half, 1/16 inch (2 mm) thick. Set aside.

Cut off the top of each tomato and reserve for garnish. With a teaspoon, scoop out the insides, leaving a shell. Blanch tomato shells in salted boiling water for 5 seconds. Using a slotted spoon, transfer tomatoes to ice water. Using your fingers, slip off tomato skins. Transfer to paper towels to drain.

Fill each tomato with one-fourth of sushi rice. Insert 2 cucumber slices and 2 Parmesan shavings on one side of rice. Whisk egg yolks in a bowl and dip outside of stuffed tomato into egg yolk to coat. Place grated Parmesan on a plate and roll the outside of each tomato in it to coat. Arrange tomatoes on individual plates and garnish with tomato lids.

To make olive oil vinaigrette: Whisk together all ingredients in a bowl until well combined. Pour 1 teaspoon vinaigrette around each tomato.

Eat with a knife and fork.

Makes 4 pieces

PARMESAN CHEESE CHIRASHI-ZUSHI IN TOMATO

sushi

Couscous inari

1 cup (8 fl oz/250 ml) warm water

1 chicken bouillon cube

1 cup (6 oz/185 g) couscous

4 shiitake mushrooms, stemmed

1 tablespoon soy sauce

1 tablespoon mirin

2 tablespoons water

4 inari (bean curd pouches)

4 whole garlic chives for tying, plus 4 garlic chives, finely chopped

4 nori strips, each 3/8 x 4 inches (1 x 10 cm)

4 teaspoons tobikko

In a small saucepan, bring water to a simmer and add bouillon cube. Stir to dissolve cube. Bring to a boil and pour over couscous in a bowl, stirring with a fork. Cover and set aside for 5 minutes. Fluff with a fork.

In a saucepan, combine mushrooms, soy sauce, mirin, and water. Bring to a simmer and cook for 5 minutes.

Open inari from cut side and using a teaspoon, fill with couscous.

Wrap a garlic chive around each inari and secure with a nori strip.

Sprinkle tobikko and chopped chives on top of each inari. Remove mushrooms from liquid, squeeze out excess liquid, then arrange on top of the couscous in each piece.

Makes 4

Grilled eggplant and carrot sushi

FOR GINGER VINAIGRETTE

$^2/_3$ oz (20 g) ginger, peeled and grated

2 teaspoons soy sauce

2 tablespoons rice vinegar

2 tablespoons olive oil

1 Japanese eggplant (aubergine)

1 large carrot, peeled and halved lengthwise

3 tablespoons olive oil

2 cups (10 oz/300 g) prepared sushi rice

(pages 20–21)

To make ginger vinaigrette: Whisk together all ingredients in a bowl. Set aside.

Cut eggplant lengthwise into 6 slices, each $^3/_8$ inch (1 cm) thick. Trim off skin from 2 slices to make narrow ribbons.

Using a vegetable peeler, slice carrot lengthwise from cut side to make 5 long, thin, wide slices. Cut 1 slice of carrot into 4 narrow ribbons.

Heat 1 tablespoon olive oil in a grill pan or a large frying pan over medium-high heat. Add eggplant slices and cook, for 2–3 minutes each side, until golden and tender. Transfer to a plate lined with paper towels. Add 1 tablespoon olive oil to pan and repeat with carrot slices.

In a small saucepan, heat remaining 1 tablespoon olive oil over low heat. Add eggplant and carrot ribbons. Cook, stirring gently, for 1 minute. Using a slotted spoon, transfer to paper towels to drain.

Using $^1/_4$ cup (1 oz/30 g) sushi rice for each, make 8 sushi oblong-shaped fingers, following the instructions on page 63. Set aside.

Place an eggplant strip on a dry work surface and place a rice ball on one end. Roll up rice ball in eggplant strip, and tie with a carrot ribbon. Repeat with remaining eggplant to make 3 more sushi. Then repeat, rolling rice balls in carrot slices and tying with eggplant ribbons, to make 4 more sushi.

Serve with the ginger vinaigrette.

Makes 8 pieces

GRILLED EGGPLANT AND CARROT SUSHI

Spicy barbecued eel in cucumber parcels

8 kombu (kelp) strips, 3 inches (7.5 cm) long and
  1 inch (2.5 cm) wide

1 teaspoon sugar

2 tablespoons rice vinegar

2 small English (hothouse) cucumbers, halved
  lengthwise

3 cups (15 oz/450 g) prepared sushi rice
  (pages 20–21)

3 oz (90 g) barbecued eel, heated and cut into
  8 crosswise slices

8 kinome (prickly ash) or sansho pepper (Japanese
  mountain pepper) sprigs

sweet-sour chili sauce for serving

Cut kombu into 8 ribbons, each ⅛ inch (3 mm) wide and 3 inches (7.5 cm) long. Cook kombu strips in boiling water for 1 minute. Combine the sugar and rice vinegar in a bowl. Add kombu strips and let sit for 10 minutes.

Using a vegetable peeler, slice cut side of cucumber lengthwise to make 16 long, thin, wide slices.

Wet your hands and take one-eighth of sushi rice and form it into a ball. Insert a piece of eel in center and form into a ball again. On a dry work surface, place 2 strips of cucumber to make a cross, and place ball on center. Lift the 4 cucumber ends to encase the rice, leaving an opening at the top. Tie a kombu ribbon around the outside to secure. Insert a kinome sprig in the top. Repeat with remaining ingredients to make 7 more pieces.

Serve with sweet-sour chili sauce.

Makes 8 pieces

Tip

Barbecued eel is available barbecued and frozen. After defrosting eel, heat until warm, about 30 seconds in a microwave and 2 minutes in an oven.

SPICY BARBECUED EEL IN CUCUMBER PARCELS

Blue cheese and sea urchin roe in an eggshell

1 English (hothouse) cucumber

4 eggs

1 cup (5 oz/150 g) prepared sushi rice
(pages 20–21)

8 pieces sea urchin roe

2 tablespoons blue cheese

1 teaspoon soy sauce

4 shiso (Japanese basil) or other herb flower
spikes

small bamboo leaves for garnish

Using a mandoline or a vegetable peeler, cut skin of cucumber into fine slices. Soak slices in a bowl of cold water.

Gently wash egg under running water. Using an egg cutter, gently cut off the top of each egg and remove the top portion of shell. Empty out the egg yolk and white. Using a strainer, gently place eggshell in a bowl of boiling water and blanch to sterilize for 5 seconds only or the shell will break. Remove and set aside.

In a small bowl, combine sushi rice, sea urchin roe, blue cheese, and soy sauce. Drain cucumber slices, and place in a shot glass. Using a teaspoon, fill an eggshell with one-fourth of rice mixture, then place eggshell in shot glass on cucumber shreds. Insert a shiso flower, and tuck a bamboo leaf in the top as garnish. Repeat with remaining ingredients to make 3 more pieces. Eat with a spoon.

Makes 4 pieces

Note on raw egg

Blanching an eggshell will sterilize it. However, eating raw or undercooked battery chicken eggs should be avoided in areas where salmonella has been a problem.

BLUE CHEESE AND SEA URCHIN ROE IN AN EGGSHELL

Habanero chili sushi

1 white onion, thinly sliced in round slices

8 tablespoons (4 oz/125 g) Japanese mayonnaise

leaves from 8 parsley sprigs, finely chopped

4 thin prosciutto slices cut into fine shreds

1/4 small habanero chili, seeded and finely chopped

1 tablespoon orange juice

2 cups (10 oz/300 g) prepared sushi rice

   (pages 20–21)

4 small cooked shrimp (prawns), shelled and

   deveined

soy sauce for serving

Soak onion slices in a bowl of cold water for 10 minutes. Drain well. In a small bowl, combine Japanese mayonnaise, parsley, prosciutto, and chili, and stir to mix. Stir in orange juice and then onion slices.

Divide sushi rice equally among 4 bowls. Spoon one-fourth of chili mixture into each bowl. Top with a shrimp.

Serve with soy sauce.

Makes 4 servings

Tip

The habanero is said to be the hottest of all chilies. Yellowish-orange in color, it is about the size of a Ping-Pong ball, but irregular in shape. If possible, wear rubber gloves when handling hot chilies, since they can linger on the skin even after repeated washing.

Cooked shrimp are available from seafood markets. To cook shrimp, boil in an uncovered saucepan of salted water until they become firm and change color, 3–5 minutes. Remove and place in iced water until cool.

soups

Kobucha soup with fu

1 small leek, including green parts, cut lengthwise
   into 4-inch (10-cm) long pieces

8 mushroom-shaped fu (decorative wheat gluten)

2 cups (16 fl oz/500 ml) water

4 teaspoons kobucha (powdered kelp tea)

4 arugula (rocket/mizuna) leaves

Slice leeks thinly and soak slices in a bowl of water for 20 minutes. In another bowl of water, soak fu for 10–15 minutes. Drain excess water from fu by hand.

In a small saucepan, bring water to a boil. Add kobucha powder and stir until dissolved. Remove from heat. Put 2 pieces of fu and some leek slices in each bowl.

Garnish with an arugula leaf.

Makes 4 servings

Tips

Fu, or dried wheat gluten, has a wide variety of shapes and sizes. It is available from Japanese and some other Asian markets.

Kobucha, made from kelp and salt, is usually drunk as a tea. It is available from Japanese markets. If unavailable, a kelp-seasoning powder may be substituted.

KOBUCHA SOUP WITH FU

Spinach-tofu rolls in wasabi-cilantro soup

FOR SPINACH-TOFU ROLLS

4 spinach leaves

3 oz (90 g) silken tofu, drained

FOR WASABI-CILANTRO SOUP

2 cups (16 fl oz/500 ml) water

1 cup (8 fl oz/250 ml) chicken broth

1 tablespoon wasabi paste

leaves from 4 cilantro (fresh coriander) sprigs

To make rolls: Blanch spinach in boiling water for 3–4 seconds. Drain and plunge into cold water. Drain in a colander and set aside.

Cut tofu into 4 slender blocks. Place a spinach leaf on a work surface and put a tofu block on top, then roll up firmly. Repeat with remaining tofu blocks and spinach. Using a knife, cut each roll in half and set aside.

To make wasabi and coriander soup: Combine water, chicken broth, wasabi and cilantro in a food processor. Process until smooth. Transfer to a medium saucepan and bring to a boil. Remove from heat. Place 2 pieces spinach-tofu roll into each of 4 soup bowls and pour the soup over.

Makes 4 servings

Grilled scallops and caviar in miso soup

12 white sea scallops without roe

1 tablespoon mirin

1 tablespoon olive oil

2 cups (16 fl oz/500 ml) water

1¹/₂ tablespoons white miso paste

4 teaspoons salmon caviar

4 scallions (shallots/spring onions), green parts
only, halved lengthwise

Place scallops on a plate and drizzle mirin over them. Heat olive oil in a grill pan or frying pan over medium-high heat. Add scallops to pan, reduce heat to low, and cook on each side until opaque. Transfer scallops to a plate and set aside.

In a medium saucepan, bring water to a boil. Reduce heat to a simmer. In a cup, mix miso paste with 1 tablespoon of the boiling water, and then pour into pot. Add scallops and cook until heated through. Do not overcook. Place 3 scallops in each of 4 bowls and gently ladle soup over them. Tie each scallion leaf in a knot and place alongside the scallops.

Makes 4 servings

Index

Guide to weights and measures

The conversions given in the recipes in this book are approximate. Whichever system you use, remember to follow it consistently, thereby ensuring that the proportions are consistent throughout a recipe.

WEIGHTS

Imperial	Metric
⅓ oz	10 g
½ oz	15 g
¾ oz	20 g
1 oz	30 g
2 oz	60 g
3 oz	90 g
4 oz (¼ lb)	125 g
5 oz (⅓ lb)	150 g
6 oz	180 g
7 oz	220 g
8 oz (½ lb)	250 g
9 oz	280 g
10 oz	300 g
11 oz	330 g
12 oz (¾ lb)	375 g
16 oz (1 lb)	500 g
2 lb	1 kg
3 lb	1.5 kg
4 lb	2 kg

VOLUME

Imperial	Metric	Cup
1 fl oz	30 ml	
2 fl oz	60 ml	¼
3 fl oz	90 ml	⅓
4 fl oz	125 ml	½
5 fl oz	150 ml	⅔
6 fl oz	180 ml	¾
8 fl oz	250 ml	1
10 fl oz	300 ml	1¼
12 fl oz	375 ml	1½
13 fl oz	400 ml	1⅔
14 fl oz	440 ml	1¾
16 fl oz	500 ml	2
24 fl oz	750 ml	3
32 fl oz	1L	4

USEFUL CONVERSIONS

¼ teaspoon	1.25 ml
½ teaspoon	2.5 ml
1 teaspoon	5 ml
1 Australian tablespoon	20 ml (4 teaspoons)
1 UK/US tablespoon	15 ml (3 teaspoons)

Butter/Shortening

1 tablespoon	½ oz	15 g
1½ tablespoons	¾ oz	20 g
2 tablespoons	1 oz	30 g
3 tablespoons	1 ½ oz	45 g

OVEN TEMPERATURE GUIDE

The Celsius (°C) and Fahrenheit (°F) temperatures in this chart apply to most electric ovens. Decrease by 25°F or 10°C for a gas oven or refer to the manufacturer's temperature guide. For temperatures below 325°F (160°C), do not decrease the given temperature.

Oven description	°C	°F	Gas Mark
Cool	110	225	¼
	130	250	½
Very slow	140	275	1
	150	300	2
Slow	170	325	3
Moderate	180	350	4
	190	375	5
Moderately Hot	200	400	6
Fairly Hot	220	425	7
Hot	230	450	8
Very Hot	240	475	9
Extremely Hot	250	500	10

First published in the United States in 2002 by Periplus Editions (HK) Lrd
with editorial offices at 364 Innovation Drive, North Clarendon, Vermont 05759 and
130 Joo Seng Road #06-01/03 Singapore 368357

LCC Card No. 2002103666
ISBN 0-7946-5008-2
ISBN 978-0-7946-5008-7

DISTRIBUTED BY

North America, Latin America & Europe
(*English Language*)
Tuttle Publishing
364 Innovation Drive
North Clarendron, VT 05759-9436
Tel: (802) 773-8930
Fax: (802) 773-6993
Email: info@tuttlepublishing.com
www.tuttlepublishing.com

Japan
Tuttle Publishing
Yaekari Building, 3rd Floor
5-4-12 Osaki, Shinagawa-ku
Tokyo 141-0032
Tel: (03) 5437-0171
Fax: (03) 5437-0755
Email: tuttle-sales@gol.com

Asia Pacific
Berkeley Books Pte. Ltd.
130 Joo Seng Road
#06-01/03
Singapore 368357
Tel: (65) 6280-1330
Fax: (65) 6280-6290
Email: inquiries@periplus.com.sg
www.periplus.com

Set in Frutiger on QuarkXpress
Printed in Singapore

First Edition
10 09 08 07 06   10 9 8 7 6 5 4

A note on eating raw fish
Fish can only be eaten raw when it is fresh. Purchase only
sashimi-grade fresh fish, following the "Choosing and
Preparing Fish and Shellfish" instructions on page 18.